BUILDING A SPECIAL COLLECTION OF CHILDREN'S LITERATURE IN YOUR LIBRARY

Identifying, Maintaining, and Sharing Rare or Collectible Items

Dolores Blythe Jones

ASSOCIATION FOR LIBRARY SERVICE TO CHILDREN

American Library Association
Chicago and London 1998

Project editor: Joan A. Grygel
Text design: Dianne M. Rooney
Cover design: Tessing Design
Composition by The Composing Room of Michigan in Cheltenham on the Macintosh Operating System using QuarkXPress 3.32.

The paper used in this publication meets the minimum requirements of American National Standard for Information Sciences—Permanence of Paper for Printed Library Materials, ANSI Z39.48-1992.∞

Library of Congress Cataloging-in-Publication Data

Building a special collection of children's literature in your library : Identifying, maintaining, and sharing rare or collectible items / Dolores Blythe Jones, editor.
    p. cm.
    Includes bibliographical references (p.   ) and index.
    ISBN 0-8389-0726-1
    1. Libraries—United States—Special collections—Children's literature. I. Jones, Dolores Blythe.
    Z688.C47B85   1998
    025.2'78088'99282—dc21   97-43144

Printed in the United States of America.

02 01 00 99 98   5 4 3 2 1

CONTENTS

Introduction

Zena Sutherland

The two books edited by Carolyn W. Field, *Subject Collections in Children's Literature* (R. R. Bowker, 1969) and *Special Collections in Children's Literature* (ALA, 1982) and the third edition edited by Dolores Jones, *Special Collections in Children's Literature: An International Directory* (ALA, 1995), have become standard texts on what special collections of children's literature exist, what areas or subjects they comprise, and where they are located.

Here the contributors add to that store of knowledge by sharing their expertise on why and how to preserve and conserve, how best to do it, and what resources exist to make doing it more efficient and more accessible to a spectrum of users. It would be difficult to think of any aspect of "why and how to establish and operate a special collection of children's literature" that these diligent and knowledgeable experts have not covered.

DianeJude L. McDowell's essay serves as an overview of special collections of children's materials, most often consisting of books but also including toys, comics, and audiovisual items. She defines the materials and the scope of such collections, giving many examples that range from those that are small and selective to such major collections of children's materials as the Lilly Library (400,000 volumes) or the International Youth Library in Munich. After consideration of the justification for establishing and maintaining such special collections, McDowell discusses their many uses and describes some of their major groups of users. In sum, the essay serves admirably as a preface to the selections that follow.

With the parameters and purposes of establishing a collection defined, John M. Kelly addresses the important topic of collection development. He stresses the importance of knowing the history of children's books and the trends and issues that affect them as well as being informed about the authors and artists who have created them. In planning a collection, he points out, one must know what to collect, one must have a detailed collection development policy, and one should know reference sources and how these differ if the collection is retroactive or contemporary. Kelly posits that it is especially useful, if it is the former, that one learn the terminology of the antiquarian book trade. The essay concludes with useful suggestions for judging prices and ordering from a catalog, with information on microformat and facsimiles and with a list of out-of-print dealers and a bibliography.

Justin Schiller's discussion of the appraising of rare and collectible children's books is remarkable both for its thorough and professional examination and for the elegance and lucidity of its writing style. In dealing with the complexities of establishing the value of a rare or desired children's book, Schiller is practical in considering details and persuasive in establishing principles that help a collector or a curator make decisions. His advice on selecting an appraiser is informed and practical; the information about price guides, auctions, and reference sources is extensive.

A model of clarity, the essay by Dolores Jones on the cataloging of special collections reminds readers that a well-organized catalog provides immediate access to all aspects of a collection's holding and that the specific needs of users must be addressed. For example, a collection serving scholars must be cataloged with their needs in mind. The essay is broad in coverage and impressively detailed and specific in the examples it provides. Jones advises using standard cataloging rules, compiling a policy manual, and establishing an authority file. Descriptions of the usefulness of the Internet and of bibliographic utilities precede a bibliography of basic cataloging references.

The arrangement, description, and cataloging of such primary source materials as manuscripts, illustrations, and correspondence are considered in the essay written jointly by Dolores Jones and Anne Lundin. A discussion of the procedures and aids that contribute to the availability of such materials includes databases, electronic resources, and descriptive standards. The material is carefully organized and clearly presented, with stress on the principles of provenance and original order. Sources for further information and illuminating examples of definitions and decisions are included, and a bibliography is provided.

As the new curator of the May Massee Collection, Mary Bogan was faced with severe preservation problems. In her essay on "Preservation and Security," she speaks with conviction of the curator's need for knowledge of techniques and speaks from experience of the help available when confronted by imminent disaster. Bogan's emphasis is on the myriad resources available to those who manage special collections. The essay is a compilation of useful—often essential—dos and don'ts that are specific either as obstacles or as remedies when there has been deterioration of materials. Both the essay and the bibliography provide access to information in various media, facts about educational programs, and sources of help through professional associations and institutions.

Margaret Maloney's focus is on the functions of special collections, which may serve as a repository, mount an outreach program, or provide a wide range of services to aid the research efforts of individual users. The author maintains a nice balance between propounding principles and goals and giving practical suggestions for provision and use of materials, for use of space, and for guarding the rights of patrons without impairing security of the collection. Her primary mandate for personnel in special collections is succinct: "to identify, acquire, make accessible, and preserve the resources appropriate to support the interest and work of their perceived clientele."

All of the preceding essays have explored such aspects of special collections of children's books as needs, procedures, acquisition policies, processing, and giving service. With few exceptions, these aspects need financial backing. In "Funding Special Collections," Karen Nelson Hoyle discusses what the priority needs are (staffing, for example), who raises funds, and how they do so. Hoyle suggests ways of achieving financial goals beyond the mandatory institutional support: volunteers, trustees, organizations with allied interests, foundations, and official supporters such as Friends groups. Fund-raising techniques vary; Hoyle gives specific suggestions for methods, for publicity, and for maximum involvement of staff, donors, and volunteers. A bibliography of sources of information complements textual citations of helpful literature.

While there have been allusions to promotion and publicity in preceding essays, in "Public Relations and Programming" by Linda Murphy and Mary Beth Dunhouse, the subject and its importance to the growth of a collection are fully analyzed. The authors emphasize the need to know the collection thoroughly and to tailor goals and objectives to the special qualities of the collection. They advocate the use of a broad range of print and electronic media— described in meticulous and extensive detail—to gain widespread and effective publicity. Also explored are such promotional activities as putting on programs (including advice on the procurement of speakers), attending professional meetings, setting up in-house exhibits, and dealing with donors.

Serenna F. Day, in the final essay, "Friends Groups," combines an effectively informal style of writing with a chronological summary that goes from why-have-a-Friends-group to a mission-accomplished! ending. Between start and conclusion is a rational, thoughtful compilation of appropriate steps to take in founding or guiding such a support group. Appreciation of group support and optimism about such a group's potential pervade Day's suggestions for avoiding problems and achieving goals.

Special Collections of Children's Materials: An Overview

DianeJude L. McDowell

As defined in the *ALA Glossary of Library Terms,* a *special collection* is "a collection of materials of a certain form, on a certain subject, of a certain period, or gathered together for some particular reason, in a library that is more or less general in character."[1] In the words of Carolyn Wicker Field, former head of children's services at The Free Library of Philadelphia, a special collection "is an in-depth collection of materials organized around a specific subject, author, illustrator, theme, or format that is made available to scholars and researchers."[2] The scope of a special collection can also be limited by time period, local interest, publisher, or language. In the case of children's special collections, the collection normally consists of materials primarily written on a juvenile level, although some resource materials written for adults are often included. These resource materials include specialized works about children's literature and library service to children as well as bibliographies, genre guides, biographical materials, guides to other special collections, and various indexes.

The word *book* has not been used to describe these materials since it is too limiting. Many children's special collections contain children's games, comics, toys, audiovisual items, and ephemera. Some collections in the most recent edition of *Special Collections in Children's Literature* include young adult materials.[3]

Sizes and Scopes of Collections

The criteria established for a children's special collection may be
very selective and may result in a very small collection. For example, according to *Special Collections in Children's Literature,* the My-
ron and Una Mae Anderson Appalachian Literature Collection at
the Davis and Elkins College Library in West Virginia contains fewer
than 200 books, the collection at the Research Center of the Betty
Hageman Memorial Library in Glen Ellen, California, houses only
first editions of works by Jack London, and the collection housed
at the Weter Memorial Library of Seattle Pacific University consists
of Bible stories.[4]

Many of the largest institutions containing children's special
collections in the United States have well over 100,000 items, which
may be housed in more than one specific collection. As noted in
Special Collections in Children's Literature, the Lilly Library at Indiana University in Bloomington houses more than 400,000 volumes,
the Children's Literature Research Collections at the University of
Minnesota includes not only the Kerlan Collection but also the Hess
Collection of dime novels and two other highly specialized collections.[5] In Philadelphia, within blocks of each other, are The Free Library of Philadelphia, with its reference and research collections of
children's literature housed in the Rare Book Department's collections (primarily pre-1837) and its Children's Special Collections
(1837 to current); the Library Company with more than 400,000 volumes; and the Rosenbach Museum and Library's Maurice Sendak
Collection.[6]

Internationally, probably the best-known and most extensive
collection is the International Youth Library in Munich. It "is the
only 'youth library' in the world that systematically collects children's literature from worldwide publishers." [7] For children's literature in Czech, the Suk Library in Prague (the Czech Republic)
houses more than 50,000 volumes and survived the "'normaliza-
tion' following the Soviet occupation of Czechoslovakia in 1968." [8]
In Japan, Tokyo has several fine collections including the National
Diet Library, a legal deposit library housing materials primarily in
Japanese from 1868 to the present. The Tokyo Kodomo Toshokan
(Tokyo Children's Library) is a private library that has as a circulating component a research collection and two special collections
of children's materials.[9] As is seen by this short list, children's special collections can be found in academic, public, private, or special libraries; they vary tremendously in scope and size; and they
can be of interest to a wide segment of society.

Need for Special Collections
in Children's Literature

Ellen Whitney, former head of the Central Children's Department of The Free Library of Philadelphia, stated that "the primary purpose of special collections of children's literature is to preserve the classics and masterpieces, as well as popular and lesser works that are out of print."[10] In the past, as circulating children's collections were weeded, many titles were lost forever. Anyone wanting a historical overview was left without primary source material. It was that concern that led Helen Sattley, then president of the Children's Services Division of the American Library Association, to appoint the Committee on the National Planning of Special Collections of Children's Books in 1964. The committee was charged with identifying, coordinating, and planning for library special collections in the field of children's literature not including general browsing collections, parent-teacher collections, or those in education materials centers.[11] The charge of the committee led to the publication of *Subject Collections in Children's Literature,* now in its third edition under the title *Special Collections in Children's Literature: An International Directory.*

A recent article in the *Times Educational Supplement* reported that Elizabeth Hammill, a children's bookseller for fifteen years in Britain, has realized that many major children's works by English authors and illustrators—England's literary heritage—have not been saved in any central source. In addition, these works cannot be found in Great Britain since many of the original materials are no longer there. The manuscripts, original art, correspondence, notes, and other materials are owned by libraries throughout the world, many in the United States. Hammill is spearheading the effort to establish a British Centre for the Children's Book. The Centre will be supported by the National lottery and focus on collecting original works by British authors and illustrators.[12] Some have blamed "the British for their past short-sightedness" in failing to collect native works.[13] Another possible reason for the short supply of these materials is that their intended audience—children—are well-known for their harsh treatment of books.

Before assuming that the situation in America is better than that in Great Britain, we need to remember that the majority of children's special collections in the United States were established relatively recently. Some of the most prestigious and thorough collections were not started until the middle of this century or later. For example, the Kerlan Collection at the University of Minnesota was founded in 1949, and the de Grummond Collection at the University of Southern Mississippi was not established until 1966. The Children's Special Collections at The Free Library of Philadelphia was begun in 1955, while the pre-1837 children's books in the Rare Book Department date from the receipt in 1947 of the Rosenbach Collection (not to be confused with the Rosenbach Museum and Library). Although the Library of Congress is not officially designated as America's national library, most people assume it is. Its Children's Literature Center was not established until 1963. Although the third edition of *Special Collections in Children's Literature* lists more than 300 institutions in the United States that have special collections devoted specifically to children's materials, many first editions, original works, and other important materials are already lost.

Uses of the Collections

Writers of books, dissertations, theses, and articles often make use of the primary source material found in children's special collections. This research often leads to the publication, even informally, of information on unexplored aspects of children's literature.[14] While attending the 1995 midwinter meeting of the American Library Association in Philadelphia, a professor examined the original Evaline Ness illustrations owned by The Free Library's Children's Special Collections for possible use in a new book. More recently, a researcher has been using variants of L. Frank Baum's *The Wonderful Wizard of Oz* in preparation for a paper he will be presenting during the centenary anniversary of the publication of this classic children's book.

Many children's special collections possess original manuscripts, editorial notes, correspondence, galleys, and other materials. By studying the accumulated material on one work, a student could determine how subtle nuances in the text were changed to make the finished work more precise. The importance of these changes can be seen dramatically in the collected documents of Lloyd Alexander in The Free Library's Children's Special Collections. Alexander would often work and rework the opening sentence or paragraph of his books. After an examination of these writing stages, readers might conclude that Alexander's purpose was to create an inescapable web, inviting to any child who would read that first page.

Children's special collections can also be used as a curriculum support base for both undergraduate and graduate courses. For many years, students at Temple University who took a course taught by Jaqueline Shachter Weiss used the collections at The Free Library of Philadelphia each semester. More recently, a particularly ambitious Drexel University student wanted to compare not only two or three versions of Cinderella but all single editions in our holdings. This past summer, a user who had difficulty finding copies of Tomie de Paola's early works was successful in locating them in the Children's Special Collections at The Free Library.

Outside the direct purview of children's literature disciplines, children's works can be used by sociologists and psychologists. They can supply "insight into the emotions and behavior of children in past eras of time."[15] On the verso, history and literature criticism now borrow heavily from psychology, sociology, and anthropology. We now have an ever-growing "cross-fertilization of disciplines."[16] Children's books can also be examined to determine how concepts and people were either developed or portrayed in literature of the past. They can document the culture of past eras with their ability to mirror life as it actually was. They also represent "the real social history of the country in which they are produced."[17] Although many of these books were not bought by libraries they still found their way into children's minds and hands. For instance, Horatio Alger's books were printed in a variety of formats to fit the strata of society—from cheap paperbacks to glorious leather-bound editions.

A collection arranged by date can serve as an overview of publishing techniques: printing fonts used, types of illustration techniques shown, binding, etc., thus helping document the history of the printed book.

At the Center for the Study of Books in Spanish for Children and Adolescents at California State University in San Marcos, you can discover books published since 1989 covering a wide range of Spanish/Latino interests. The Center now includes activities such as "training seminars [and] workshops for teachers of bilingual education."[18]

Professional storytellers often use children's special collections, sometimes to get a feel for what has already been done and at other times for source materials. Collections with older books can be particularly useful if the patron is searching for material that is in the public domain.

Use of children's special collections is not limited to the

scholar or student. A frequent but most difficult type of question is from someone seeking a book or story fondly remembered from childhood. The Kerlan Collection fielded one such query from a chemistry professor, a member of the National Academy of Science, who was searching for a variant of *The Little Red Hen* that differed from the standard version.[19] A question posed to the staff of The Free Library came from a patron whose only clue was that the story she wanted to share was in a series of books named after gems. Since most of our folklore is housed together, a search of the shelves in the j398.4 classification revealed the Jewel Series by Ada Maria Skinner. The names of the books in the series were chosen to be analogous to a broad category of stories, so that "emerald" contains stories about nature; "pearl," winter; "amber," autumn, etc. The satisfied patron was able to photocopy the story she was seeking.

In this same vein, patrons come in to reread books they loved as children. Some wonder why this or that particular book held them in such fascination, while others question the book's literary worth—was the story really as wonderful as they remember it? Finding answers to these types of questions is often most rewarding, since the patron "has been looking for this book all over for years" and for some measure of time, the rediscovered book has transported them to another time and place.

At The Free Library, the collections have been used to give background information for a local TV program on where the phrase "mad as a hatter" originated. We also helped the same program with a feature on the pony roundup, using an early printing of Marguerite Henry's *Misty of Chincoteague*. What we originally thought was a unique use came one year in early fall. A participant in the upcoming Mummers' Day Parade came in to do research. It turned out that three different groups were using us that same year with all of them swearing us to secrecy.

Since there aren't enough copies and most special collections could not afford to purchase originals, republication of long out-of-print materials is of growing significance. Some are done as reprints, others as replicas, and the best (such as Lothar Meggendorfer's movable toy books) as beautifully done facsimiles. Morrow with its "Books of Wonder," Grosset & Dunlap's "Illustrated Junior Library" books, and others have been releasing classics with illustrations done by N. C. Wyeth, Jessie Willcox Smith, Charles Robinson, John Tenniel, W. W. Denslow, and others. These works with their original illustrations gloriously reproduced have added a new dimension to children's circulating collections. Viking has recently issued "The Whole Story" series, including Kipling's *The Jungle Book,* Jack London's *The Call of the Wild,* and Jules Verne's *Around the World in Eighty Days.* This series is filled with illustrations, maps, and wonderfully informative captions that explain words, phrases, and give background details for the reader. Today's publishers have also issued classics by L. Frank Baum, Mark Twain, Edgar Allan Poe, and Aesop illustrated by contemporary artists such as Michael Hague, Barry Moser, and others. Running Press has published several classics using source material from Children's Special Collections at The Free Library of Philadelphia including Frances Hodgson Burnett's *A Little Princess,* Anna Sewell's *Black Beauty,* and Louisa May Alcott's *Little Women.* All of these books have found a new home in the hearts of today's children, but that would not have been possible without the foresight to rescue and protect the originals.

Authors use the collections to do historical research to ensure the accuracy of their text. They may also use the collection as "an inexhaustible source for researching the background of novels, short stories, or nonfiction books."[20] Grateful for the help she was given, Esther Forbes bequeathed royalties from the sale of her books, including *Johnny Tremain,* to the American Antiquarian Society in Worcester. [21]

Special Collections and Child Patrons

Although established for the collection of children's materials, children's special collections are generally not open to use by children. Most collections are for adult use only, with smaller parts restricted to scholarly use. However, there are at least two libraries that have explored the direct use by children under very controlled conditions. Beverly Hills Public Library has introduced fifth graders in local public schools to children's special collections with a program focusing on Aesop's fables. Using duplicates, facsimiles, later editions, and contemporary works, students have embarked on a study of a myriad of subjects: book collecting, printing techniques, history of illustration, and literary analysis, among others.[22] At the Mazza Collection, children are enticed into a love of reading and art appreciation by seeing the original art from children's books and by hearing from the artists themselves. [23]

At The Free Library of Philadelphia, the late Rusel Silkey of the Rare Book Department mesmerized grade school students each year by showing them marvels such as cuneiform tablets, a book with a reversible fore-edge painting, and, of course, "Grip"—the raven who may have inspired Poe's famous poem. One of the events offered by the Central Children's Department as part of the 1996 summer reading program was "Treasures and Tales." The audience was captivated with a mix of storytelling and historical discussion accompanied by toy and movable books. The children were transported to another time and place and were amazed to discover that not very long ago videotapes didn't exist.

The Future

Computers, the World Wide Web, virtual libraries, and digitization of images are already here or just on the horizon. The Internet is already directly influencing the use of children's special collections. At The Free Library, reference questions have been transmitted to Children's Special Collections through the general information department. The de Grummond Collection has an excellent Web site (http://www.lib.usm.edu/degrumm.htm), and the site for Children's Special Collections of The Free Library of Philadelphia is under construction (http://www.library.phila.gov.htm). With today's sophisticated search engines, millions of people throughout the world not only will have instant around-the-clock access to information about the collections but also will be able to view some subject matter directly.

Notes

1. *ALA Glossary of Library Terms* (Chicago: American Library Assoc., 1971), 31.
2. Carolyn Wicker Field, "The Role of the Special Collection in Children's Literature," *Illinois Libraries* 67 (Jan. 1985): 5.
3. Dolores Blythe Jones, ed., *Special Collections in Children's Literature: An International Directory,* 3d ed. (Chicago: American Library Assoc., 1995), 96.
4. *Special Collections,* 7, 32, 94.
5. *Special Collections,* 32, 49–50.
6. *Special Collections,* 82–5.
7. Janet R. Thompson and Richard A. Thompson, "A Literary Treasure House for Teachers: The Internationale Jugendbibliothek in Munich," *Journal of Reading* 37, no. 5 (Feb. 1994): 386.

8. Ivana Hutarova, "Suk's Library of Children's Literature," *Bookbird* 33, no. 3/4 (fall/winter 1995–1996): 97.

9. *Special Collections*, 211–12.

10. Ellen Whitney, "Special Collections of Children's Literature: A Justification for Their Support," *Top of the News* 43, no. 1 (fall 1986): 73.

11. Field, 5.

12. Elaine Williams, "Childhood Treasure Trove Slips Away," *Times Educational Supplement* no. 4179 (2 Aug. 1996): 5.

13. Daniel Zalewski, "The Atlantic Paper Chase," *The Higher/The Times Higher Education Supplement* (5 May 1995): B7.

14. John M. Kelly, "Collections of Historical Children's Books: Development and Access," *Illinois Libraries* 67 (Jan. 1985): 10.

15. Whitney, 73.

16. Anne Lundin, "Text and Context: Special Collections and Scholarship," *College and Research Libraries* 50, no. 5 (Sept. 1989): 554.

17. Eugene F. Provenzo, Jr., "A Note on the Darton Collection, Special Collections, Teachers College, Columbia University," *Teachers College Record* 84, no. 4 (summer 1983): 929.

18. L. Erik Bratt, "A Bilingual Children's Book Center in California," *Bookbird* 33, no. 3/4 (fall/winter 1995–1996): 100–1.

19. Karen Nelson Hoyle, "Treasure Houses to Share: Children's Literature Special Collections," *Journal of Youth Services in Libraries* 6, no. 4 (summer 1993): 406.

20. Whitney, 73.

21. Hoyle, 403.

22. Rita Lipkis, "Books in the Classroom: Young Hands on old Books," *The Horn Book Magazine* 69, no. 1 (Jan.–Feb. 1993): 115.

23. Zoe Ingalls, "The Art of Illustrating Children's Books," *The Chronicle of Higher Education* 41, no. 19 (20 Jan. 1995): B6.

Further Reading

ALA Glossary of Library Terms. Chicago: American Library Assoc., 1971.

Avery, Gillian. "The Baldwin Library: An English Tribute." *The Horn Book Magazine* 58 (Aug. 1982): 446–51.

Balas, Janet. "Special Libraries and Special Librarians on the Internet." *Computers in Libraries* 16, no. 6 (June 1996): 46–7.

Bock, Susie R. "History of Children's Literature Collections at the University Libraries [The University of Colorado at Boulder]." *Colorado Libraries* 20, no. 1 (spring 1994): 40–1.

Chodorow, Stanley A., and Lynda Corey Claassen. "Academic Partnership: A Future for Special Collections." *Journal of Library Administration* 20, no. 3/4 (Mar./Apr. 1995): 141–8.

Dequi, Henry C. "What's So Special about Special Collections." *Illinois Libraries* 67 (Jan. 1985): 14–17.

Dickinson, Donald. "A Career in Collecting: Edgar Oppenheimer." *Wilson Library Bulletin* 63, no. 6 (Feb. 1989): 52–4.

Eliassen, Meredith. "From Dime Novels to Disney." *School Library Journal* 41, no. 7 (July 1995): 19–21.

Field, Carolyn Wicker. "The Role of the Special Collection in Children's Literature." *Illinois Libraries* 67 (Jan. 1985): 5.

Hoyle, Karen Nelson. "Special Collections of Children's Literature in an American Academic Setting." Paper presented at The IFLA Annual Conference, Manila, 18–23 Aug. 1980. ERIC ED208817 IR009412.

———. "Treasure Houses to Share: Children's Literature Special Collections." *Journal of Youth Services in Libraries* 6, no. 4 (summer 1993): 400–8.

Ingalls, Zoe. "The Art of Illustrating Children's Books." *The Chronicle of Higher Education* 41, no. 19 (20 Jan. 1995): B6.

Jones, Dee. "The de Grummond Collection: A Multipurpose Resource for Librarians, Teachers, and Scholars." *The Horn Book Magazine* 71, no. 1 (Jan./Feb. 1995): 102–5.

Jones, Dolores Blythe, ed. *Special Collections in Children's Literature: An International Directory.* 3d ed. Chicago: American Library Assoc., 1995.

Kelly, John M. "Collections of Historical Children's Books: Development and Access." *Illinois Libraries* 67 (Jan. 1985): 10–14.

"Lasting Impressions: Illustrating African-American Children's Books" Exhibit at The Jane Voorhees Zimmerli Art Museum, Rutgers, The State University of New Jersey, 15 Sept.–17 Nov. 1996.

Lee, Sul H., ed. *The Role and Future of Special Collections in Research Libraries: British and American Perspectives.* Binghamton, N.Y.: Haworth, 1993.

Lenz, Millicent, and Gillian McCombs. "The Pleasure Reading Books of Yesteryear." *Wilson Library Bulletin* 62, no. 8 (Apr. 1988): 15–16.

Lipkis, Rita. "Books in the Classroom: Young Hands on Old Books." *The Horn Book Magazine* 69, no. 1 (Jan./Feb. 1993): 115–18.

Lundin, Anne. "Text and Context: Special Collections and Scholarship." *College and Research Libraries* 50, no. 5 (Sept. 1989): 553–6.

Maloney, Margaret Crawford. "Public Trust: Special Collections of Children's Materials." In *Lands of Pleasure: Essays on Lillian H. Smith and the Development of Children's Libraries,* edited by Adele M. Fasick, Margaret Johnston, and Ruth Osler, 143–51. Metuchen, N.J.: Scarecrow, 1990.

Mundell, Lynn. "Minnesota's Center for Research on Children's Literature." *The Chronicle of Higher Education* 36, no. 27 (21 Mar. 1990): B7.

Provenzo, Eugene F., Jr. "A Note on the Darton Collection, Special Collections, Teachers College, Columbia University." *Teachers College Record* 84, no. 4 (summer 1983): 929–34.

"Reports from the Great Collections." *Bookbird* 33, no. 3/4 (fall/winter 1995–1996): 77–111.

Ryan, Michael T. "Developing Special Collections in the '90's: A Fin-de-siècle Perspective." *Journal of Academic Librarianship* 17, no. 5 (Nov. 1991): 288–93.

St. John, Judith. "The Osborne Collection of Early Children's Books: Highlights in Retrospect." *The Horn Book Magazine* 60 (Oct. 1984): 652–60.

Thompson, Janet R., and Richard A. Thompson. "A Literary Treasure House for Teachers: The Internationale Jugendbibliothek in Munich." *Journal of Reading* 37, no. 5 (Feb. 1994): 386–8.

Traister, Daniel. "Garbage or Treasure: The Case for Acquiring Rare Books." *The Chronicle of Higher Education* 39, no. 19 (13 Jan. 1993): A48.

Weathers, Inalea. "Special Collections in Public Libraries: Enhancing Community Service." *Wilson Library Bulletin* 61 (May 1987): 23–5.

Whitney, Ellen. "Special Collections of Children's Literature: A Justification of their Support." *Top of the News* 43, no. 1 (fall 1986): 73–83.

Williams, Elaine. "Childhood Treasure Trove Slips Away." *Times Educational Supplement* no. 4179 (2 Aug. 1996): 5.

Zalewski, Daniel. "The Atlantic Paper Chase." *The Higher/The Times Higher Education Supplement* no. 1174 (5 May 1995): 18.

2
Collection Development

John M. Kelly

A solid background in the field of children's literature is essential to the successful development of a special collection. The librarian or collector who is aware of the history, issues, and trends as well as the significant authors, illustrators, and publishers of children's books will be able to make astute collecting decisions. Such knowledge may be gained through formal programs, classroom instruction, or independent reading. A number of library schools and departments of English and education offer courses and specialized degrees in children's literature, including Simmons College (Boston), Hollins College (Virginia), Illinois State University (Normal), and Eastern Michigan University (Ypsilanti). In addition, short-term noncredit courses in a variety of pertinent subjects are available through institutes, workshops, and summer programs. An excellent example is the University of Virginia's Rare Book School that provides excellent one-week courses in historical children's literature and related subjects.

Specialized Reading

Finances, logistics, time, or other factors may prevent you from pursuing a formal education in children's literature. However, motivated librarians or collectors can become knowledgeable about their chosen subspecialty within children's literature through broad and specialized reading.

For the study of historical children's books, a key title is F. J. Harvey Darton's *Children's Books in England: Five Centuries of Social Life*. Darton's survey, originally issued in 1932, is still the classic assessment of the field. Brian Alderson has done a masterful job of incorporating the results of modern scholarship into the third edition, as well as adding a well-chosen bibliography and incisive notes. *Written for Children: An Outline of English Language Children's Literature* by John Rowe Townsend provides a good overview, as does Paul Hazard's *Books, Children and Men*.

The history of American children's literature from 1621 to 1922 is discussed in Gillian Avery's *Behold the Child*. Illustrators and their illustrations, past and present, are discussed in *The Bright Stream: A History of Children's Book Illustration* by Joyce Irene Whalley and Tessa Rose Chester and in Barbara Bader's exhaustive survey, *American Picturebooks from Noah's Ark to the Beast Within*. Two standard textbooks, both recently updated, are *Children's Literature in the Elementary School* by Charlotte Huck and Zena Sutherland's *Children & Books*.

The parameters established for a particular special collection will dictate specialized titles to add to the basic reading list. Is the collection limited to the literature of a particular country, author, illustrator, or publisher? Is genre, format, subject, or time period the determining factor? If so, choose your references accordingly.

What to Collect

After becoming familiar with the field of children's literature and establishing the parameters of the collection, the major issue becomes what to collect. Regardless of its scope, there are three key elements that must be present in a well-developed collection. First and foremost, you should collect the landmark and cornerstone authors and titles. To be truly successful in meeting this objective, financial resources must be adequate for the established collection parameters. A focus on eighteenth-century children's literature will require more monetary support than a collection emphasizing post-World War II picture books. Second, the collection should acquire those titles that will round out and strengthen its holdings as well as attract researchers to its facility. Typically, such titles are not those commonly found at most institutions. For example, a scholar conducting research on the career of Maurice Sendak is not likely to need access to your copy of *Where the Wild Things Are*. But he or she will be excited to examine closely *Atomics for the Millions* (1947), a scarce science text that Sendak illustrated while still a high school student! Third, strong holdings of reference tools, bibliographies, review journals, directories, specialized collection catalogs, and other secondary works are a must.

Collection Development Policy

It is very important to have a written record of all decisions. This document will become your collection development policy, a structured guideline to assist in the selection process. If your collection is limited to alphabet books, you must resist the urge to purchase that wonderful new counting book. If you collect pop-up books, will you add a lift-the-flap book? What about the book, cassette, and stuffed animal multimedia kit that is ever so appealing—does it belong in a collection previously restricted to books? Decisions similar to these will constantly test the validity and strength of your collection development policy. (See Appendix A at the end of this chapter for a sample collection development policy.)

Contemporary Collection Development

If a special collection acquires current in-print children's books, you should scan regularly the review section of pertinent journals to locate desirable titles. A short list includes *Book Links, Booklist, Bulletin of the Center for Children's Books, CCL/Canadian Children's Literature, Children's Book Review Index, Growing Point, Horn Book Magazine, Horn Book Guide to Children's and Young Adult Books, Junior Bookshelf, Kirkus Reviews, MultiCultural Review, Publishers Weekly, Quarterly Black Review of Books, School Library Journal,* and *VOYA/Voice of Youth Advocates* as well as occasional issues of the *New York Times Book Review* and *TLS, The Times Literary Supplement.* Obviously, if the focus of the collection is international, you should review European, Canadian, Australian, and other specialized sources.

Online review sources include Notes from the Windowsill, Carol Hurst's Children's Literature Site, Parents' Choice, The Hungry Mind Review, and The Scoop: Children's Books Online. Current addresses for these sites as of this writing are listed at the end of this chapter.

Titles worthy of selection are also discussed in scholarly articles in publications such as *Children's Literature, Children's Literature Association Quarterly, Bookbird, Lion and the Unicorn, Children's Literature in Education, Signal,* and *The Five Owls.* Regrettably, two highly regarded titles, *Phaedrus* (1973–1988) and *Die Schiefertafel* (1978–1986), have ceased publication. However, back issues of these two titles may be analyzed profitably for retrospective collection development. Issued quarterly, *Children's Literature Abstracts* provides access to a wide range of information on recently published secondary sources and critical studies.

Retrospective Collection Development

When the focus of the collection requires retrospective rather than contemporary selection, a different approach is needed. Most of the items desired for the collection are out of print and require different methods of acquisition. Working with out-of-print, or antiquarian, booksellers who specialize in children's books is the most common approach to developing a retrospective collection. Many dealers issue catalogs that list items currently available. These catalogs have traditionally been available through the mail, but increasingly it is possible to find the full text and even illustrations on World Wide Web sites.

Fortunately, there are a large number of booksellers who specialize in children's books. Distinguished booksellers such as Justin Schiller and Daniel Hirsch emphasize material that is often quite rare and relatively expensive. Carol Docheff, Helen Younger of Aleph-Bet Books, Elizabeth Moody, and Joanne Reisler are also highly regarded, but they trade mainly in twentieth-century books that are less scarce and usually less costly. A selective listing of American antiquarian booksellers is appended to this chapter. Other dealers may be located in printed reference sources such as the *American Book Trade Directory,* the *AB Bookman's Yearbook,* and *Literary Market Place.*

Online sources include home pages for the Antiquarian Booksellers Association of America, the International League of Antiquarian Booksellers, the American Booksellers Association, and newsgroup sources for buying and selling books. Internet addresses, or URLs, for these sources are appended to this chapter.

Booksellers' Catalogs

Before trying to understand the entries in catalogs of antiquarian booksellers, it is advisable to become familiar with the terminology of the book trade. The best reference work available is John Carter's *ABC for Book Collectors.* Although arranged in an encyclopedic format, the commentary is so lucid, witty, and informative that Carter's book may be read joyously as a text from cover to cover. Even experienced booksellers and librarians frequently refer to this helpful book.

In an attempt to standardize the subjective art of grading the condition of books, the antiquarian book trade has adopted the following standardized categories of description: "as new," "fine," "very good," "good," "fair," "poor," "ex-library," "book club," and "reading copy." The best definitions available for these terms are published frequently in issues of *AB Bookman's Weekly.*

Most dealer catalogs will provide information regarding the abbreviations used in their catalogs and also policies regarding their terms of sale. Careful reading of this information will provide much-needed answers to frequent questions.

Librarians should also be familiar with the basics of bibliography to fully understand the world of first editions, duodecimos, and association copies. An excellent text is *A New Introduction to Bibliography* by Philip Gaskell. Topics covered include printing type, composition, paper, imposition, presswork, binding, illustration, bibliographical description, and textual bibliography. The section on the identification of format is extremely useful when attempting to determine whether a volume is a folio, quarto, octavo, etc.

Armed with an understanding of the book trade and bibliography, you can now turn to the booksellers catalogs. These catalogs vary greatly in format and content. Some are produced on inexpensive paper without illustrations and are stapled together. These catalogs generally give very brief listings and descriptions. Other dealers issue handsomely bound catalogs with detailed descriptions, commentaries, bibliographical references, and full-color illustrations. Some of these well-produced catalogs, such as Justin Schiller's *Realms of Childhood,* have become standard reference works that are consulted by librarians, scholars, and other booksellers. A number of dealers now have their catalogs online as well.

How does the buyer determine which booksellers are the most reliable, with a fairly priced stock of desirable books? Following are four areas of consideration to keep in mind while examining a catalog.

1. Does the bookseller describe the book accurately? Has the book been examined and collated by the bookseller? If the book lacks a textual leaf or an illustrated plate, the description must indicate the deficiency.
2. If the bookseller states that a copy for sale is a first edition, is it in fact the first edition? Some dealers will cite copies of Kate Greenaway or Beatrix Potter titles as first editions, when in fact this is not the case. Reputable booksellers will cite *first edition* only when there is positive evidence.
3. Does the bookseller use bibliographical references properly? Frequently, dealers will state that a book is "not in" a certain standard bibliography as supporting evidence of its scarcity. If the title for sale is an American picture book published in 1930, it is inappropriate to cite "not in Osborne" as the Osborne Collection catalog lists only pre-1910 British children's books. Conversely, a bookseller who properly uses extensive bibliographical citations is likely to be quite knowledgeable in rare books as well as children's literature.
4. Is the bookseller a member of the Antiquarian Booksellers Association of America or a similar organization? Members of such organizations generally have to achieve and maintain certain standards of performance.

DESIDERATA FILE

When dealing with booksellers, it is very beneficial to have a list of out-of-print titles (commonly referred to as a desiderata list) that you would like to add to the collection. It is important to consider these lists as fluid and not static, as titles will be added and deleted over time. Remember that wanting to add an out-of-print title does not automatically mean that you will find a copy! Some desired titles may be located within weeks of being entered into a desiderata file, other titles will take years to locate, and still other elusive titles will never be acquired.

When a catalog arrives, review its contents as soon as possible, since in most instances booksellers have only one copy of a listed title in stock. If you delay, the book you desire might already be sold by the time you place your order.

No two librarians follow the same procedure when examining

catalogs and ordering books, but the following routine has worked successfully for the author. Scan the catalog quickly and circle the items that sound appealing. Then, read the catalog again, this time going through more thoughtfully and deliberately. On this reading, you will circle additional items and possibly delete a few titles initially circled. Then carefully check the remaining circled items against the library's current cataloged and uncataloged holdings.

PRICES

Ultimately, the most difficult issue is whether the price asked by the bookseller is a fair one. There is no easy answer to this complex question. The world of antiquarian booksellers is not as patterned, nor as structured, as the world of vendors and publishers. However, it is governed by the basic laws of supply and demand. You must also rely on experience when assessing the appropriateness of prices. Having access to such references tools as *Bookman's Price Index* and *American Book Prices Current* is certainly useful. Back files of catalogs from reputable booksellers can also be most helpful when evaluating the cost of out-of-print books.

It is quite possible that Dealer A will offer a title for $50 and Dealer B will offer the same book for $75. Why the difference? A point to consider is the relative condition. Dealer B's copy might be in fine condition with a dust jacket, while Dealer A's copy is only in good condition and is lacking the dust jacket. Is a dust jacket worth $25 or more? Dust jackets are an integral feature of children's books and are highly valued. In many instances, illustrative and textual material found on the dust jacket is not repeated in the book. They are very desirable accompaniments to books published in the late nineteenth and early twentieth centuries. In particular, post-1950 children's books originally issued with dust jackets should be acquired with the jackets present whenever possible.

ORDERING

When you have finally found a book that is needed in your collection and the price is right, it is time to place the order. Telephone, send a fax, or contact the dealer by E-mail when placing an order from a bookseller's catalog. Sending an order card to the library's acquisition department or even writing to the bookseller are almost sure ways of *not* getting the book that you desire! Depending on the fiscal guidelines of your institution, you may call, reserve the book, and send a purchase order, or you may instruct the bookseller to ship the book with an invoice. Acquisitions departments and business offices need to be reminded that invoices from booksellers need to be paid promptly, usually within thirty days. It is unfair to expect a small business to wait months for payment.

Online Sources

The Internet now offers several alternatives to the traditional booksellers catalog. Bibliofind is a Web site that allows you to scan the stock of second-hand and rare-book sellers around the world with the ease of a single search. Interloc, an electronic marketplace, provides an online database and matching service that connects buyers and sellers of books, photographs, manuscripts, prints, illustrations, and related materials.

Advertising Want Lists

Many librarians and collectors do not have the time to study numerous dealer catalogs. An alternative or supplementary procedure is to advertise your want list. The advantages to this method are that it is not as time-consuming as reviewing catalogs, and it allows the collector to select the best offer from the multiple quotes that are received from booksellers. Obviously, the objective is to acquire the copy that is the lowest priced and in the best condition. There are two major publications that print lists of books wanted by libraries. Booksellers scan these lists and forward quotes to libraries for titles they have located. *AB Bookman's Weekly* has the advantage of being reviewed by a very large number of booksellers, but its relatively high advertising fees often make it prohibitive for institutional libraries. A less costly alternative is *The Library Bookseller* that, unfortunately, is scanned by fewer dealers. Once it subscribes to *The Library Bookseller,* a library may submit "books wanted" lists at will, without additional charges. The want lists are printed approximately one month after submission.

Auctions

Another method employed by many private collectors and some institutional libraries for children's book acquisition is auction sales. Major auction houses that periodically feature sales of children's books are Sotheby's (London), Swann Galleries (New York), Christie's (South Kensington, England), and Christie's East, (New York). Initiating subscriptions to catalogs of important sales from the leading auction firms is a good way to learn about future offerings. Carefully prepared auction catalogs may also be useful as future reference tools. Although some librarians have placed bids directly at auctions (or sent bids by mail), institutions tend to rely on a trusted bookseller to act as an agent. A final word about prices realized at auctions: Two collectors participating in the same sale and coveting the same book will likely inflate the hammer price. Therefore, be cautious when reviewing and interpreting auction sales figures.

Facsimiles

Another means of acquiring antiquarian titles is through the purchase of facsimiles. Children's collections frequently acquire facsimiles for a variety of reasons. First, the acquisition of a facsimile copy of John Newbery's *A Little Pretty Pocket-Book* allows access to a title that would be virtually impossible to locate via the rare-book market. Second, when a collection holds a fragile original copy as well as a facsimile, the facsimile will likely be adequate for use by a significant percentage of patrons, thereby saving on wear and tear of the original edition. Third, some facsimiles are of great use to researchers because of the valuable commentaries, notes, and bibliographies.

Several facsimile series of historically significant children's books have been published. A superb series is the wonderfully edited Juvenile Library published by Oxford University Press. Another recommended set is the sumptuously printed Osborne Collection of Early Children's Books issued by Bodley Head in the early 1980s. Another set, ultimately disappointing, is Classics of Children's Literature 1621–1932, published by Garland. The garish bright yellow cloth bindings and the frequently sparse and inadequate editorial commentary detract from this series' potential usefulness. Still, there are some titles such as Benjamin Harris's *The Protestant Tutor* (1679), James Janeway's *A Token for Children* (1676), and Thomas Boreman's *The Gigantick History of the Two Famous Giants and Other Curiosities in Guildhall, London* (1740), that are rarely encountered today save for the Garland printings.

Microformat

Brief mention must be made of collections of children's books available in microformat. A. S. W. Rosenbach's *Early American Children's*

Books was released by KTO Microform in 1975. Chadwyck-Healey, as a part of its monumental series *The Nineteenth Century,* has a subsection entitled *Literature Specialist Collection, Part 2: Children's Literature,* edited by John Barr of the British Library. A most-eagerly awaited set, UMI's *The Opie Collection of Children's Literature,* is now partially available. As of early 1997, twenty units had been published, with another twenty units to be published at the rate of four per year. More than 20,000 titles from the great personal collection of Iona and Peter Opie, many rare or even unique, are now available to scholars on microfiche. The original collection is now housed at the Bodleian Library of Oxford University.

Donations

Curators of institutional special collections of children's books also hope to acquire some of their material as gifts from donors. Donors usually want to contribute to established programs that have a proven track record. Potential donors may be interested in answers to questions such as

> Does the institution have a solid collection (or collections) already in place?
> Has research been published that relied on the holdings of the collection?
> Does the institution distribute brochures, newsletters, or other publications?
> Does it disseminate publicity or participate in outreach programs such as symposiums, seminars, or book festivals?
> Has the institution supported exhibitions, catalogs, and guides?
> Does the institution provide a professional staff, knowledgeable in both children's literature and special collections?
> Do the facilities have adequate security and a climate-controlled environment?
> Are contributions processed or cataloged and made available to scholars?

It is crucial that an institution make a favorable impression during the first contact with a potential donor. A warm letter detailing the specific interest, accompanied by promotional items, is generally a good first contact. But for many potential contributors, nothing can take the place of a personal visit. Few truly magnificent private collections of children's books are left. The collections of such figures as Elisabeth Ball, Ruth Baldwin, and Lloyd Cotsen have found good homes at noted academic institutions. Still, for many institutions the key to developing special collections of children's books lies in strong and continuing ties with donors and potential donors.

What to Purchase

The focus now turns to the specifics of titles and areas to be purchased. The author cautiously offers the following advice to those of you who are charged with the selection of items to be added to collections of children's literature.

Titles published early in the careers of major authors and illustrators are especially desirable. Once a writer has "established" himself or herself, subsequent titles are generally printed in larger quantities, given greater publicity, and collected regularly shortly after publication. Books illustrated by Kate Greenaway before her landmark *Under the Window* was published in 1879 are generally encountered less frequently than those released in the 1880s and 1890s. Many libraries collecting modern American picture books have most of the titles written and illustrated by Ezra Jack Keats after the publication of his famous work, *The Snowy Day,* in 1962. Yet, how many institutions have extensive holdings of the books he illustrated in the 1950s? These early titles are frequently the books that researchers need to examine to construct a complete and thorough portrait of an author or illustrator.

Another important category for potential collecting is that of significant, although virtually unknown, authors and illustrators. How do you learn about such creators? Here, you must look primarily to our leading authorities of children's books, the specialist booksellers. Knowledgeable dealers will emphasize and highlight in their catalogs authors and illustrators who have been ignored by the standard histories and bibliographies. As an example, B. and N. Parker are virtually unknown author/illustrators, yet together they produced a remarkable series of oblong quarto picture books from 1906 to 1927.

In addition to favorite authors and illustrators, there are a number of publishers whose works have become quite influential and collectible. Early publishers such as Isaiah Thomas, Benjamin Tabart, John Marshall, and William Darton are generally better remembered than the writers they published. Important studies and bibliographies of significant publishers such as John Newbery and John Harris have been printed, and undoubtedly the number of these studies will increase. Even collections focusing on twentieth-century children's books have a number of significant publishers to consider collecting, including Harlin Quist, William R. Scott, the P. F. Volland Company, and The Saalfield Publishing Company.

Invariably, many collections desire to develop a strength in the books created by the famous "gift book" illustrators of the early twentieth century, namely Arthur Rackham, Edmund Dulac, Kay Nielsen, Willy Pogany, and Harry Clarke. It is true that the limited, and even the trade editions, of the works of these noted illustrators are glorious examples of book illustration and production. Keep in mind, however, that early editions of these illustrated books are quite expensive, and fine collections of these "gift books" are relatively common. Instead, why not concentrate on collecting the work of talented illustrators such as Jessie King, Clara Tice, Lawson Wood, W. W. Denslow, A. B. Frost, Horace Knowles, Henry L. Stephens, Fanny Cory, Bessie Pease Gutmann, and Graham Robertson, who produced many fine books and yet are little collected or studied compared with Arthur Rackham.

A large number of collections naturally place a high emphasis on the acquisition of award-winning books. Having a strong collection of Newbery Medal and Caldecott Medal recipients is standard fare. Yet, how many collections have complete holdings of the Newbery Honor Books? It is surprising how difficult some of these titles are to acquire. Sadly, largely because of ignorance, these desirable books have been weeded from many libraries in recent years. On a more positive note, however, booksellers have been quite successful in locating these elusive books for many libraries and private collectors.

Developers of collections often use standardized lists or bibliographies, for example Jacob Blanck's *Peter Parley to Penrod,* as acquisition guides. This is an acceptable practice, but librarians are encouraged to explore new themes and uncharted territory. Scholarly study in children's literature is a relatively recent and virgin field. In contrast to the American Civil War or William Faulkner, very few children's literature topics have been thoroughly researched. For every Lewis Carroll or Beatrix Potter, there are literally hundreds of authors, illustrators, publishers, themes, and time periods that have been ignored or have received scant attention. For example, a checklist of Volland publications needs to be issued. An in-depth study of Madame d'Aulnoy is desperately needed. John

Marshall's principal authors—Dorothy and Mary Ann Maze Kilner, Ellenor Fenn, Lucy Peacock, and Sarah Trimmer—must be analyzed. So much remains to be learned about children's magazines. No book-length work has appeared on W. H. G. Kingston in more than forty years. Catherine Sinclair's books have received scant treatment. Further examples could be cited exhaustively.

To be truly successful, the developer of a special collection in children's literature must cultivate a sense of what will be the areas of future scholarly interest and collect accordingly. One such area is children's books published during the Great Depression era. Surprisingly, there were many beautiful books produced during the stricken 1930s. Why? Scholars will need to examine the authors, illustrators, and publishers of this period to answer that question. For every recognizable name from this era, such as Lois Lenski, a talent such as Fern Bisel Peat has been forgotten. Most children's books published in this era, although not plentiful, may be acquired fairly inexpensively. Another area of predicted future interest is the large format (quarto or folio) picture book published from the 1890s to the 1940s. Little-known illustrators like Mary Frances Ames, Grace Drayton, Agnes Richardson, and Zhenya Gay produced a wide array of visually appealing and imaginative books.

Collection development of special collections in children's literature is an exciting and satisfying occupation. Because the field is still comparatively young, one is continually learning about unknown authors, talented illustrators, significant publishers, and undercollected themes and genres. There is a unique feeling of accomplishment when a title that has been desired for years is finally acquired! Not every collection can attain the international status of the Osborne Collection in Toronto or the International Youth Library in Munich, but many high-quality children's literature collections exist and will continue to prosper. Other new and innovative collections will be developed in the coming years.

Further Reading

Children's Books

Boreman, Thomas. *The Gigantick History of the Two Famous Giants and other Curiosities of Guildhall, London.* With a preface by Michael H. Platt. New York and London: Garland, 1977.

Eidinoff, Maxwell Leigh, and Hyman Ruchlis, with illustrations by Maurice Sendak. *Atomics for the Millions.* New York: Whittlesey House, [1947].

Greenaway, Kate. *Under the Window: Pictures and Rhymes for Children.* London and New York: George Routledge & Sons, [1879].

Harris, Benjamin. *The Protestant Tutor.* With a preface by Daniel Cohen. New York: Garland, 1977.

Janeway, James. *A Token for Children.* With a preface by Robert Miner. New York: Garland, 1977.

Keats, Ezra Jack. *The Snowy Day.* New York: Viking Pr., 1962.

Newbery, John. *A Little Pretty Pocket-Book.* A facsimile with an introductory essay and bibliography by M. F. Thwaite; 1st American ed. New York: Harcourt, Brace & World, [1967]; London: Oxford Univ. Pr., 1966.

Sendak, Maurice. *Where the Wild Things Are.* New York: Harper & Row, 1963.

Periodicals

AB Bookman's Weekly. Clifton, N.J.: AB Bookman Publ., 1948– .

AB Bookman's Yearbook. Clifton, N.J.: AB Bookman Publ., 1954– .

American Book Prices Current. Washington, Conn.: Bancroft-Parkman, 1894– .

American Book Trade Directory. New Providence, N.J.: R. R. Bowker, 1915– .

Book Links. Chicago: American Library Assoc., 1991– .

Bookbird. Baltimore, Md.: Morgan State Univ. in association with the International Board on Books for Young People, 1963– .

Booklist. Chicago: American Library Assoc., 1905– .

Bookman's Price Index. Detroit: Gale Research, 1964– .

Bulletin of the Center for Children's Books. Champaign, Ill.: Graduate

School of Library and Information Science of the Univ. of Illinois, 1947– .

CCL/Canadian Children's Literature. Guelph, Ont.: Canadian Children's Pr., 1975– .

Children's Book Review Index. Detroit: Gale, 1976– .

Children's Literature. Battle Creek, Mich.: Children's Literature Assoc., 1972– .

Children's Literature Abstracts. Austin, Tex.: Children's Libraries Section of the International Federation of Library Assocs., 1973–.

Children's Literature Association Quarterly. Battle Creek, Mich.: Children's Literature Assoc., 1976– .

Children's Literature in Education. New York: Human Sciences Pr., 1970– .

The Five Owls. Minneapolis, Minn.: Five Owls, 1986– .

Growing Point. Northampton, Eng.: Margery Fisher, 1962– .

Horn Book Guide to Children's and Young Adult Books. Boston: Horn Book, 1989– .

Horn Book Magazine. Boston: Horn Book, 1924– .

Junior Bookshelf. Thurstonland, Eng.: Marsh Hall, 1936– .

Kirkus Reviews. New York: Kirkus Assoc., 1933– .

The Library Bookseller. Berkeley, Calif.: Scott Saifer, 1945– .

Lion and the Unicorn. Baltimore, Md.: Johns Hopkins Univ. Pr., 1977– .

Literary Market Place. New Providence, N.J.: R. R. Bowker, 1940– .

MultiCultural Review. Westport, Conn.: GP Subscription Publs. 1992– .

New York Times Book Review. New York: New York Times, 1896– .

Phaedrus. Boston: Phaedrus, 1978–1986.

Publishers Weekly. New York: Cahners Publ. Group, 1872– .

Quarterly Black Review of Books. New York: Quarterly Black Review of Books, 1993– .

Die Schiefertafel. Hamburg, Ger.: E. Hauswedell, 1978–1986.

School Library Journal. New York: Cahners Publ. Group, 1954– .

Signal: Approaches to Children's Books. Stroud, Eng.: Thimble Pr., 1970– .

TLS, The Times Literary Supplement. London: Times Supplements, 1902– .

VOYA/Voice of Youth Advocates. Metuchen, N.J.: Scarecrow, 1978– .

Reference Books

Avery, Gillian. *Behold the Child: American Children and Their Books 1621–1922.* Baltimore, Md.: Johns Hopkins Univ. Pr., 1994.

Bader, Barbara. *American Picturebooks from Noah's Ark to the Beast Within.* New York: Macmillan, 1976.

Blanck, Jacob. *Peter Parley to Penrod : A Bibliographical Description of the Best-Loved American Juvenile Books.* New York: R. R. Bowker, 1938.

Carter, John. *ABC for Book Collectors.* With corrections, additions, and an introduction by Nicolas Barker. 7th ed. New Castle, Del.: Oak Knoll, 1995.

Darton, F. J. Harvey. *Children's Books in England: Five Centuries of Social Life.* 3d ed. revised by Brian Alderson; Cambridge, Eng. and New York: Cambridge Univ. Pr., 1982.

Gaskell, Philip. *A New Introduction to Bibliography.* 3d impression, first published in 1972, reprinted with corrections in 1974 and 1979. Oxford, Eng.: Clarendon, 1979.

Hazard, Paul. *Books, Children and Men.* Translated by Marguerite Mitchell. 4th ed. Boston: Horn Book, 1975.

Huck, Charlotte S., and others. *Children's Literature in the Elementary School.* 6th ed. Madison, Wis.: Brown & Benchmark, 1997.

Rosenbach, A. S. W. *Early American Children's Books 1682–1847.* Millwood, N.Y.: KTO Microfilm, 1975.

Schiller, Justin. *Realms of Childhood: A Selection of 200 Important Historical Children's Books, Manuscripts, and Related Drawings.* New York: Justin Schiller, 1983.

Sutherland, Zena. *Children & Books.* 9th ed. New York: Longman, 1997.

Townsend, John Rowe. *Written for Children: An Outline of English Language Children's Literature.* 6th American ed. Lanham, Md.: Scarecrow, 1996.

Whalley, Joyce Irene, and Tessa Rose Chester. *The Bright Stream: A*

History of Children's Book Illustration. 1st U.S. ed. Boston: D. R. Godine, 1994, ©1988.

Internet Sites

American Booksellers Association
   http://www.bookweb.org

Antiquarian Booksellers Association of America Homepage
   http://www.abaa-booknet.com

Bibliofind
   http://www.bibliofind.com

Carol Hurst's Children's Literature Site
   http://www.crocker.com/~rebotis

The Hungry Mind Review
   http://www.bookwire.com/hmr

Interloc
   http://www.interloc.com

International League of Antiquarian Booksellers
   http://www.booknet-international.com/ilab

Newsgroup for sale of books
   rec.arts.books.marketplace

Notes from the Windowsill
   http://www.armory.com/~web/notes.html

Parents' Choice
   http://family.starwave.com/reviews/pchoice

The Scoop: Children's Books Online
   http://www.Friend.ly.Net/Scoop

APPENDIX A

Collection Development Policy
for a Special Collection of Children's Literature
at a U.S. University

PURPOSES OF THE COLLECTION

1. To meet the research needs of scholars in a variety of fields including library science, education, English, art, history, sociology, philosophy, psychology, and human development.

2. To meet the undergraduate and graduate educational requirements of the university and other similar institutions. Classes in library science, education, English, art, history, sociology, foreign languages, theater, and counseling psychology are among the disciplines supported through tours, lectures, and individualized reference service.

3. To provide a working model of a special collection of rare books, manuscripts, and illustrations for the education of undergraduate and graduate library science students.

4. To provide an outreach service to public and private schools and libraries in the community and surrounding areas through tours and lectures.

5. To act as a resource for both the university and local community in matters such as children's literature, literacy, exhibits, library issues, and related topics.

MONOGRAPHS—GENERAL GUIDELINES

Means of Acquisition
Published books are acquired through purchase, donation, and to a limited degree, transfer from other library collections.

Language Coverage
Primarily English, but the collection currently holds works in a large number of languages.

Chronological Coverage
No restrictions; currently 1530 to the present.

Geographical Coverage
Primarily the United States and the United Kingdom, although prominent authors and illustrators from Canada, Australia, and New Zealand are collected.

Limited coverage of non-English speaking countries.

Types of Materials

Books and magazines for preschool children through young adults.

Monographs, selection tools, secondary sources, and dissertations.

Reprints and microformat where appropriate, both hard cover and soft cover formats are acceptable.

Areas of Focus

- Aesop and other fabulists, historical and contemporary
- Kate Greenaway materials, historical and contemporary
- Significant contemporary authors, including American, British, Australian, and Canadian
- Significant contemporary illustrators, including American, British, Australian, and Canadian
- Historical children's books 1770–1850, primarily American and British
- Newbery and Caldecott Medal winners and Honor Books; Carnegie and Greenaway Medal titles; equivalent awards in Australia and Canada
- Batchelder Award winners
- Emerging trends in children's and young adult literature
- Informational books
- Concept and ABC books, both historical and contemporary
- Series books from late 19th and early 20th centuries
- Titles issued by important or unique publishers
- Nineteenth-century English and American children's magazines
- Children's authors and illustrators from [name of state]; books set in [name of state]
- Significant children's authors and illustrators from [area of the country]
- Fairy tales and folklore, both historical and contemporary
- Early 20th-century American illustrators
- Toy, pop-up, and movable books
- Reference books, professional literature, criticism, secondary sources, exhibition catalogs, auction catalogs, and bibliographies important to the study of children's literature

Exclusions and Limitations for Purchased Materials

- Audiovisual formats
- Contemporary series books such as Nancy Drew and the Hardy Boys
- Artifacts, toys, coloring books, paper dolls, etc.
- Media tie-ins such as Care Bears and Garfield
- Mass-market titles found in grocery stores and discount chain stores

Selection Criteria

- Favorable book review in recognized source
- Significance of author, illustrator, publishers, etc.

- Citation in standard reference sources, selective bibliographies, and other secondary sources
- Importance of subject matter or genre
- Connection to existing holdings

ORIGINAL MATERIALS—GENERAL GUIDELINES

Means of Acquisitions
Currently, original materials are acquired only through donation. It should be noted that in the earlier years, funds were available for purchase.

Language Coverage
Primarily materials written in English.

Chronological Coverage
No restrictions, currently mid-19th century to the present.

Geographical Coverage
Emphasis is on the United States and the United Kingdom, although materials from other parts of the world are not excluded.

Types of Materials
Manuscripts, typescripts, proofs, galleys, original illustrations, paintings, preliminary sketches, dummies, press sheets, publisher correspondence, artifacts and ephemera, personal memorabilia, reviews, fan mail, royalty records, and other related materials.

Areas of Focus
- Manuscripts, typescripts, galleys, proofs, and other materials related to contemporary fiction and nonfiction written for an audience up to age 18.
- Original illustrations, sketches, dummies, press sheets, and other illustrative materials from published children's and young adult books. Special emphasis is placed on increasing our holdings of contemporary American illustrators.
- Publisher correspondence, reviews, fan mail, and other memorabilia related to the publication of children's books.
- Examples of materials from all stages of the creative process.
- Memorabilia, records, and ephemera related to organizations and events important in the field of children's literature.
- Manuscripts and related materials from secondary sources relevant to the study of children's literature.

Exclusions and Limitations
Manuscripts for books published for the adult audience. Exceptions are manuscripts for adult books by children's authors and secondary sources that support the study of children's literature.

Policy revised [date].

APPENDIX B

Dealers of Children's Out-of-Print Books

Marion F. Adler Books
Marion F. Adler
P. O. Box 627
Stockbridge, MA 01262
(413) 298-3559

Aleph-Bet Books
Helen and Marc Younger
218 Waters Edge
Valley Cottage, NY 10989
(914) 268-7410
Fax: (914) 268-5942
E-mail: alephbet@IX.netcom.com
www.clark.net/pub/alephbet

AnMar's Children's Series Books
A & M Carpentieri
1295 Campus Dr.
Berkeley, CA 94708
(510) 376-1573
Fax: (510) 376-1573

Arch Books
Ruth P. Hendrickson
5916 Drew Ave. S
Minneapolis, MN 55410
(612) 927-0298
E-mail: archbook@winternet.com
www.winternet.com/~archbook

Banbury Cross
Judy Gutterman
992 Oakdale Rd. NE
Atlanta, GA 30307
(770) 373-3511

Bookfinders International
Elizabeth Wessels
701 Gervais St.
Columbia, SC 29201
(803) 252-1589
Fax: (803) 736-0028

Books of Wonder
Peter Glassman
132 Seventh Ave. (At 18th St.)
New York, NY 10011
(212) 989-3270
Fax: (212) 989-1203
E-mail: BooksWon@ix.netcom.com

Bookstall
Henry and Louise Moises
570 Sutter St.
San Francisco, CA 94102
(415) 362-6353
Fax: (415) 362-1503

Bromer Booksellers
Anne and David Bromer
607 Boylston St. at Copley Square, 2nd Fl.
Boston, MA 02116
(617) 247-2818
Fax: (617) 247-2975
E-mail: BOOKS@BROMER.COM

Cattermole—20th Century Children's Books
Jane and Bill McCullam
9880 Fairmount Rd.
Newbury, OH 44065
(216) 338-3253
Fax: (216) 338-1675
E-mail: bill.mccullam@pcohio.com

Childhood Companions
Laurie McGill
1209 Northwest Hwy., Ste. 139
Garland, TX 75041-5899
(972) 271-6750
Fax: (972) 271-6750

Children's Book Adoption Agency
Barbara and Bill Yoffee
9921 Capitol View Ave.

Silver Spring, MD 20910
(301) 565-2834
Fax: (301) 585-3091
E-mail: kids_bks@interloc.com

Cohen Books & Collectibles
Joel and Linda Cohen
P. O. Box 810310
Boca Raton, FL 33481-0310
(407) 487-7888
Fax: (407) 487-3117
E-mail: btgx08a@prodigy.com

R. Crandall Books
R. Crandall
5093 Paradise Dr.
Tiburon, CA 94920
(415) 435-3325

Curiouser & Curiouser
Susan Steinman
P. O. Box 274
Santa Fe, NM 87504
(505) 988-5840

Ursula C. Davidson Books
Ursula C. Davidson
134 Linden Lane
San Rafael, CA 94901
(415) 454-3939
Fax: (415) 454-1087
E-mail:
        71324.2302@compuserve.com

Carol Docheff, Bookseller
Carol Docheff
1390 Reliez Valley Rd.
Lafayette, CA 94549
(510) 935-9595

Dower House
Anne G. Swindells
11191 Westheimer, #876
Houston, TX 77042
(713) 785-6113
Fax: (713) 785-6113

Drusilla's Books
Drusilla and Pen Jones
859 N. Howard St.
Baltimore, MD 21201-4696
(410) 225-0277
Fax: (410) 321-4955

Ann Dumler Books
Ann Dumler
645 Melrose
Kenilworth, IL 60043
(847) 251-2034
Fax: (847) 251-2044

Enchanted Books
Susan Weiser Liebegott
2435 Ocean Ave., Apt. 6J
Brooklyn, NY 11229
(718) 891-5241

First Edition of Hickory
Marcia R. Simmons
2421 N. Center St., Ste. 304
Hickory, NC 28601
(704) 327-6315
Fax: (704) 327-3925
E-mail: 72550,3206@compuserve

Doris Frohnsdorff
P. O. Box 2306
Gaithersburg, MD 20886
(301) 869-1256

Daniel Hirsch Fine & Rare Books
Daniel Hirsch
P. O. Box 5096
Chapel Hill, NC 27514
(919) 542-1816
Fax: (919) 542-1817
E-mail: rhirsch@InterServ.com

Hobbyhorse Books
S. C. and A. C. Aroldi
P. O. Box 591
Ho-Ho-Kus, NJ 07423
(201) 327-4717
Fax: (201) 760-1238
E-mail: saroldi@styx.ios.com

Illustration House, Inc.
96 Spring St., 7th Fl.
New York, NY 10012-3923
(212) 966-9444
Fax: (212) 966-9425
E-mail: illushse@interport.net
http://www.interport.
    net/~illushse

Susan J. Klein, Bookseller
Susan J. Klein
4431 Calle de Farrar
San Jose, CA 95118
(408) 978-5497
Fax: (408) 265-1528
E-mail: KleinBooks@aol.com

Gail Klemm Books
Gail Klemm
P. O. Box 518
Apple Valley, CA 92307
(619) 242-5921
Fax: (619) 242-5921

Kendra Krienke
Kendra Krienke and Allan Daniel
230 Central Park West
New York, NY 10024
(212) 580-6516
Fax: (201) 930-9765

Loganberry Books
12633 Larchmere Blvd.
Cleveland, OH 44120
(216) 795-9800

Jean S. McKenna Books
Jean S. McKenna
10 Longview Terrace
Beverly, MA 01915
(508) 922-3182
Fax: (508) 922-3182

Barbara Mader Children's Books
Barbara Mader
1833 Randolph Ave., #2
St. Paul, MN 55105
(612) 690-2439

Marvelous Books
Dede Kern
P. O. Box 1510
Ballwin, MO 63022
(314) 458-3301
Fax: (314) 273-5452
E-mail: marvelous@interloc.com

Dorothy Meyer
10751 S. Hoyne Ave.
Chicago, IL 60643
(312) 233-3368

**Elizabeth Moody Children's
  Books**
Elizabeth Moody
P. O. Box 327
Windham, CT 06280
(203) 423-2156

My Bookhouse
Dan Griffin and Cher Bibler
27 S. Sandusky St.
Tiffin, OH 44883
(419) 447-9842

Edward D. Nudelman
P. O. Box 20704
Broadway Station
Seattle, WA 98102
(206) 367-4644
Fax: (206) 367-4644

Ramelle Onstott Children's Books
Ramelle Onstott
6489 S. Land Park Dr.
Sacramento, CA 95831
(916) 428-5030

Page Books
Maggie Page
P. O. Box 233
Kingston, AR 72742
(501) 861-5831

Pomander Books
Suzanne Zavrian
P. O. Box 30

211 W. 92nd St.
New York, NY 10025
(212) 749-5906

RPM Books
Bob Matteson
104-29 Jamaica Ave., 2nd Fl.
Richmond Hill, NY 11418
(718) 441-6208

Jo Ann Reisler, Ltd.
Jo Ann and Donald L. Reisler
360 Glyndon St. NE
Vienna, VA 22180
(703) 938-2967
Fax: (703) 938-9057
E-mail: reisler@clark.net
www.abaa-booknet.
        com/usa/reisler

Charlotte F. Safir
1349 Lexington Ave, Apt. 9B
New York, NY 10128-1513
(212) 534-7933

Justin G. Schiller, Ltd.
Justin G. Schiller
135 E. 57th St., 12th Fl.
New York, NY 10022
(212) 832-8231
Fax: (212) 688-1139
E-mail: childlit@maestro.com
http://www.abaa-booknet.
        com/alldlrs/ma/10022jus.html

**Myrna Shinbaum Books
  and Book Themes**
Myrna Shinbaum and Ellen Rubin
P. O. Box 1170 Madison Sq. Sta.
New York, NY 10159-1170
(212) 982-5749
Fax: (914) 725-3053
E-mail: popuplady@aol.com

Sister Brute Books
P. O. Box 777-262
Alamo, CA 94507

(510) 552-2865
Fax: (510) 743-0381

Barbara E. Smith Books
Barbara E. Smith
P. O. Box 1185
Northampton, MA 01061
(413) 586-1453

Elizabeth Stone Gallery
Elizabeth Stone
580 N. Woodward Ave.
Birmingham, MI 48009
(313) 647-7040

Ten Eyck Books
Arthur and Catherine Ten Eyck
P. O. Box 84
Southboro, MA 01772
(508) 481-3517

Treasures from the Castle
Connie Castle
1720 N. Livernois
Rochester, MI 48306
(810) 651-7317

Well Read Books
Bea Coryell
2 Folly Field Ct.
Cold Spring Harbor, NY 11724
(516) 692-8257

Wonderland Books
Allan Friedman
7511 Fairmount
El Cerrito, CA 94530
(510) 528-8475
E-mail: alland@dnai.com
www.dnai.com/~alland

Elaine Woodford Bookseller
Elaine Woodford
323 Hillside Lane
Haddonfield, NJ 08033
(609) 354-9158
Fax: (609) 354-9709

3

Appraising Rare and Collectible Children's Books

Justin G. Schiller

Many factors contribute to an increased awareness and interest in old books intended for the use of children: the worldwide formation of specialized research institutes, the frequency of major exhibitions devoted to this subject (often accompanied by impressive and well-illustrated catalogs), the development during the past few decades of several important children's book collections (both public and private), and the resources of surfing the Internet where search engines will locate specialized home pages of favorite authors and illustrators. Clearly there has been a gradual legitimizing of children's books as worthwhile collectibles, and each volume we possess (or want to possess) now comes under careful scrutiny.

Gone are the days (back in the 1970s) when dealers would casually point to a dark dusty shelf in the rear of their shop or auction houses would be selling such collections by the cartonful. Indeed, international auctions are regularly scheduled several times a year devoted to the field of children's books and related artwork, and we can barely keep up with reading newly issued catalogs of old and rare juvenile books produced by booksellers from all over the globe. Thus, it is not surprising to find general confusion as to the monetary value of these books that not so long ago could have sold for a few dollars and now fetch prices well into three and four figures.

Factors Affecting Value

Regretfully, there is no easy formula for establishing the current fair market value of a rare or desired children's book, and several factors must be equated: *influence* the publication of this book had on its genre, *literary merit* of its text, *graphic appeal* of its illustrations, and overall *physical condition* in relation to the availability of other copies of the same book, along with the well-known formula for all types of collectibles—*supply* and *demand.* When considering the original audience for whom these books were intended, it is easier to understand why fewer copies are likely to have survived than comparable works of adult literature printed at the same time . . . even though we might assume that books for children were produced in larger quantities.

The Internal Revenue Service (Regulation 66-49) requires that any claims for tax-benefit donations be accompanied by a written appraisal from a recognized authority and that these appraisals be based upon the "fair market value" of an item—the price at which a book or drawing or manuscript could be expected to change hands between a willing seller and a willing buyer on the open marketplace. Certainly it sounds easy enough, but how are such values actually determined?

In providing an authoritative appraisal, a thorough knowledge of the subject matter is necessary—which includes the ability to place material into a historic perspective. It often requires being able to judge a book's importance in the overall scheme of children's literature and to establish its relative rarity and desirability within a hypothetical hierarchy. An original drawing by Randolph Caldecott or Walter Crane is of serious value once the authenticity of it has been established, but the correct value of one drawing is not necessarily equal to the value of any other drawing by the same artist. And so it is with books. All of the juvenile titles published in London or New York during any particular year are not of identical value, and we can understand that. However, it must also follow, we can seldom find two copies of an old book in identical condition. Therefore, the value of one copy of a book is often less or more than the value of another copy of the very same edition because of subtle physical differences in their survival.

Sometimes even the relevant importance of a particular title may not be obvious. The 1810 London reprint of *Gamma Gurton's Garland* is a collection of unillustrated nursery rhymes previously published in 1784 and 1799, and it only becomes more enticing when we realize that this 1810 version contains substantial additions—including the very first printing of the poems "Humpty Dumpty" and "Little Bo Peep." Likewise, Lowell Mason's *Juvenile Lyre* (Boston 1831) on first appearance seems to be a rather modest textbook for school and home use in learning to play a musical instrument or to sing in harmony; that it still is, but it also prints the earliest musical setting to Sarah Hale's poem "Mary Had a Little Lamb," first published as a text the previous year. On quick observation, and without finding any pictures inside, we might discount these titles as being rather dull, but each is quite rare and relatively valuable. In today's market the first would easily fetch $1,000 and probably more, depending on condition, while a copy of the second has recently fetched $750. Neither is a staggering price but certainly more than anyone could ever imagine by looking at them without knowing their peculiarities.

As we begin to consider the value of books published during the late nineteenth and early twentieth centuries, we must also start to consider if the book being evaluated ever had a dust jacket and whether other copies of this book are known in dust jacket. The concept of these protective wraparounds dates back to the 1820s in England when publishers first became aware that books could get damaged (during storage or in transit) before being sold by the retailer; cardboard sleeves or simple paper covers were sometimes provided, with just enough printing to identify the specific book title. Eventually these jackets became more decorative, and at times were even specially designed by the artist with an illustration not otherwise reproduced on the front cover or inside the book itself. Famous dust-jacketed books include Washington Irving's 1848 first separate printing of *Rip Van Winkle* illustrated by the American artist Felix O. C. Darley (here the dust jacket was simply a large paper-printed envelope that contained the book), Lewis Carroll's 1876 *Hunting of the Snark,* and Arthur Conan Doyle's 1892 *Adventures of Sherlock Holmes.* With the last two works, the front cover design was reprinted in a slightly simpler form. A fragmented dust jacket for a first edition of *Wonderful Wizard of Oz* (1900) by L. Frank Baum was purchased in 1972 at Sotheby Parke Bernet on behalf of a private collector. The book was in the earliest binding state, but the presence of its partial dust jacket was not even detailed by *American Book Prices Current.* It fetched $800. When it sold at auction twenty years later (Swann Galleries, Epstein sale), the partial dust jacket was a featured element of the description. Of course interest in collecting this important title had magnified significantly during the interim, so it fetched $20,900. Edgar Rice Burrough's 1914 *Tarzan of the Apes,* first edition, fine copy, may be worth about $2,500 for a handsome copy in original cloth, first binding, but it increases to more than $35,000 when coupled with a near-perfect original pictorial dust jacket. The relative values may be all askew, but at least you should realize these possibilities if you are going to appraise or price anything collectible.

Hierarchy within Printing History

Along with identifying a book for its textual or illustrative importance as well as for the added value of such component parts as original dust jacket, perhaps the most important part of any appraisal is to accurately identify the book's position in the hierarchy of its printing history. Therefore, we must briefly discuss descriptive bibliography and the essential meaning of the most commonly used bibliographical terms. Here the confusion mounts, for textbook definitions do not always "translate" to their applicable understanding in book collecting. The words *edition, impression, issue,* and *state* are very important to comprehend by way of their variables since they help describe the priority of publication. The monetary value often follows that which is the uncorrected state of the first issue of the first impression of a first edition.

Generally speaking, *edition* describes "all copies of a book printed from the same setting of type at one time or another," which thus allows for the subcategory *impression:* "all copies of a book printed at one specific point in time." A number of impressions from the same setting of type can be produced over a period of many years, especially through stereotyping and photoreproduction methods. Technically speaking they still can be called part of the same edition since the body of the type (except, perhaps, for its preliminaries) has not been altered. About twenty years ago an innocent collector had recently bought a very fine copy of Melville's *Moby Dick* (New York 1863), original cloth, purchased in good faith as a "first edition, later state" for $2,500. As such, it is an extremely rare book representing the third American printing of Melville's text—but twelve years after the first printing. The collector knew that the first edition was printed in 1851 but thought of this as a remainder issue from the same sheets with a later dated title page; he was wrong. Instead, what he had purchased was a reprint from stereotyped plates actually done in 1863. Such a mistake is hard to accept, regardless of it being an honest misunderstanding (or lack of knowledge) on the part of the bookseller who sold it to him. Today this collector has become both hesitant and paranoid, seldom trusting any dealer longer than a few months and periodically selling off whatever he has assembled over short time periods without ever developing his collecting instincts.

If we carry the above analogy a bit further, we could imagine calling a facsimile reprint of a Gutenberg Bible or a 1623 first folio Shakespeare a first edition, later state! Copies of such replicas (facsimiles) have been relatively inexpensive, but perhaps the day will come when we will see such reproductions actually cataloged and sold in that manner. The suggestion is a fantasy, but one we should nevertheless guard against.

The next subcategory to define is the word *issue:* "that part of an edition offered for sale at one particular time, or as a consciously planned unit." It is quite normal for the first impression of an edition of a book to be distributed by means of several different issues, each essentially the same except for a different title page: perhaps one giving the imprint of a New York publisher for distribution in the United States while the regular version has a London imprint. We may even find "Colonial" editions printed in England but for sale only to member countries in the Commonwealth.

Whereas the term *issue* is usually determined by the publisher after a book is printed, variant *states* occur before publication. This is usually caused when an error is discovered during the printing of a book and the press run is stopped long enough to correct the mistake. Sheets printed before the error was noticed constitute the uncorrected state, while sheets printed afterward are the corrected (or second) state. Even if the sheets are bound up at the same time and issued simultaneously, those containing the uncorrected text will probably be more desirable—and, in effect, more valuable.

Pricing

Assuming that the material being appraised is adequately identified and researched, its value still cannot be determined until a price structure for the same or similar items can be established. Once again, experience becomes the best source for this information. The price that one bookseller may put in his or her catalog is only as valid as the capabilities of that dealer to determine a correct market price—and an asking price is not necessarily a successful selling price! Conversely, prices realized at auction indicate only the highest price level a particular group of people were willing to bid under the conditions of a specific sales day and in combination with their own levels of expertise, the expertise of the auction house cataloger who described this material in print, and even with reference to the desirability of other items also being offered for sale at the same time.

Perhaps the most difficult concept to understand is that there is more than one correct value for almost everything; the "right price" for an item must be duly pegged, depending upon the approach or context in which that item is being considered. As an example, one of John Newbery's most famous nursery juveniles is his 1761 *Newtonian System of Philosophy* by Tom Telescope. As a first printing of an early and rare Newbery title, it has one value. It is worth somewhat more money as an early science work promoting the esteemed principles of Sir Isaac Newton, and there may still be another criterion for evaluating this little book by collectors of antique toys since the text deals chiefly with the mechanics of spinning tops, gyroscopes, and so forth. Each price is quite valid, and perhaps nowadays prices are even moving somewhat closer together than has been true in the past. However, we might still find differentials of many hundreds of dollars between them.

Children's books written by Charles Lamb sell primarily as rare literature rather than as children's books, and as such their marketability could be five or ten times greater than the value given to a comparable work with similar appeal but written anonymously. The second edition of Mary Wollstonecraft's *Original Stories from Real Life* (London 1791) is also multifaceted: as a text for children based upon the author's experience as a governess, as a specimen of feminist literature, but (most importantly) as a work newly illustrated by William Blake. It is a good collector or librarian who can appreciate this sliding range of values beyond the immediate focus or context, as oftentimes the more unusual and interesting titles have overlapping interests and one may have to be pursued on more expensive grounds than simply in its context as children's literature. It is this spectrum of values that also allows one knowledgeable bookseller to buy from another colleague—with no one feeling embarrassed that a mistake had been made in pricing a book but simply recognizing the variables of a different marketplace where the criteria for pricing within one context can be altered and reevaluated when the same book is offered for sale by someone else.

Costs of Appraisals

Assuming that you do locate a qualified specialist to do an appraisal, the costs for doing such work can be prohibitive when put alongside the actual value being appraised. Therefore, some appraisers charge a percentage of the determined value as their fee—usually from 1½ percent to 3 percent. Under those conditions the objectivity of such an appraisal must be questioned, for the higher the value, the higher the fee being charged. An alternative is to pay for time actually spent on the appraisal. Any responsible professional would likewise advise from the start if the material being reviewed does not seem relatively justified for time-estimate costs in doing this work.

Depending on the appraiser's qualifications and experience, you might expect to find rates being charged from $75 to $300 per hour plus expenses. Keep in mind that the specialist who charges $300 per hour (the same fee you must now expect to pay a top lawyer) is not necessarily more expensive than someone charging much less money per hour. An experienced appraiser might complete the work within a half-day, while someone with less familiarity with the material could take a full week for research and still not end with the same expert result. The appraiser must be able to research and identify that which is unknown on a personal level (or verify any statements accompanying the material if they are not from an acknowledged authority) and assess the relative value of the items being appraised within a justified criterion.

In paying the per-hour fee charged by an expert appraiser, you are partially paying that amount as security that the appraisal will be correct and what is being appraised will be properly described. However, a per-hour fee seldom compensates a high-powered professional for time away from regular bookshop activity, lost sales, delay in reading catalogs, consideration of purchases from other sources, and the general halting of business operations. (When I do such work, I generally bring along an associate who prepares the material to be appraised and records details for items that I need to verify afterward; this results in an additional charge of $125 per hour, but it actually saves me and the client extra time charged at the higher fee since my assistants are quite highly trained and will work rapidly in recording necessary information.)

In searching out an appraiser, it is always best to begin by providing a detailed checklist for author, title, place of publication, publisher, date (as it appears on the title page, not on the copyright page), and illustrator, unless the appraiser will already be familiar with the specific collection being evaluated. With such a list the appraiser will know if he or she is qualified to deal with these matters. Any good dealer or appraiser will also verbally indicate if these items appear to be of a collectible value that is worth the cost of an appraisal (as mentioned earlier). But it should be noted that such informal work is only that, and under these circumstances the appraiser cannot verify the completeness of a book without actually going through it and counting its pages and its illustrations. This requires collation and should always be done in a written report on any item with serious potential value. Therefore, we return again to a formal appraisal, whether it is for one book or an entire library. The cost of appraisal time is usually counted by work "on premises" as well as time in doing additional research and preparing a written report. Additional expenses incurred during any appraisal, such as travel and lodging, are generally charged at cost.

Guidelines for Estimates

Following are a few guidelines as well as warnings for the collector or librarian who may want to estimate the value of children's books. These notes can be used in preparing for a more-thorough analysis by a professional appraiser or may prove sufficient for the purpose and thus not require any additional work.

Using Reference Books and Bibliographies

Reference books and bibliographies can be an important source of information, but in selecting them you should also be aware of their inherent limitations. Always read the prefatory remarks to know what criteria were used in assembling details, and try to determine the level of expertise of those who compiled the research. Such books are only as good as the authority behind them. With modern advances in communication, the bibliographer is no longer restricted to access to one or two particular sources but can locate and inspect other recorded examples through photocopies, microfilm, the increasingly popular fax machines, and most recently, the electronic highway of the Internet (where database files can be searched and professional collations and descriptions accessed virtually twenty-four hours a day from all over the world). There is greater sophistication nowadays in keeping books in their original binding compared to the earlier practice of having everything rebound in attractive gilt leather. It may even be more costly to restore an original binding than to have it completely recovered, but in doing so we preserve the integrity of the book and likewise have one additional element for use in comparison with other copies. The techniques used today in collecting data for research would have been unimagined a half century ago.

Before the year 1950 few scholarly works were published in the field of early children's books. For British juvenile books, the most reliable and comprehensive survey was F. J. Harvey Darton's *Children's Books in England* (1932)—made far more useful by a fiftieth anniversary third edition revised and edited by Brian Alderson, who verified and updated the text bibliographically with information discovered during the past fifty years. Well-researched but directed toward a more-popular audience are Percy Muir's *English Children's Books 1600 to 1900* and Joyce Irene Whalley's *Cobwebs to Catch Flies;* both are well-illustrated, somewhat chatty, and provide listings for additional reading.

All the books by Iona and the late Peter Opie are fully authoritative and correctly documented, based upon their own examination of actual books and a most remarkable cross-reference card file that they have been compiling since the 1940s. Their *Oxford Dictionary of Nursery Rhymes* (1951, and still in print) provides a significant contribution to the printing history of 550 separate rhymes (many with alternate readings) going back to the seventeenth and early eighteenth centuries. Their *Classic Fairy Tales* (1974) details the origins of two dozen fairy stories followed by an unadulterated text for each tale cited.

Another useful work, seldom given the recognition it deserves, is William Targ's *Bibliophile in the Nursery.* It contains twenty-four articles written by collectors and researchers, including a complete reprint of the 1954 descriptive catalog for the Pierpont Morgan Library's first children's literature exhibit and Professor William H. Bond's documented study comparing the 1865 and 1866 printings of *Alice's Adventures in Wonderland* previously published in the *Harvard Library Bulletin.*

As for American children's books, there have been fewer scholarly references that can be relied upon for accuracy—the majority being produced more from nostalgia and naiveté than from solid research. The best-known and still quite useful early work is

Dr. A. S. W. Rosenbach's *Early American Children's Books* (1933), but readers should realize its limitations as well as know its virtues. This is strictly a descriptive catalog of a randomly selected 816 items published in America between 1682 and 1836. Lavishly produced by The Southworth Press with hand-colored illustrations after the originals, it physically describes books in the Rosenbach collection, but readers should not totally rely on its commentary. Rosenbach inherited the majority of these items from his uncle Moses Polock, a bookseller in mid-nineteenth century Philadelphia. Polock had bought up and safely stored large groupings of unsold children's books from publishing houses that gradually went out of business. In some cases there were up to 800 duplicate copies of single titles. Rosenbach proceeded to market them by producing this rather elaborate catalog, which illustrated them intermixed with additional books of the period. This descriptive catalog was a limited edition sold to subscribers, and a few weeks after someone might buy a copy of this catalog a formal letter would be sent from The Rosenbach Company saying that the Doctor was disposing of items from his collection and offering for sale some thirty-six titles—with specific references to the published catalog. These duplicate books were not expensive, and no undue advantage was taken except the unspoken but implied rarity of this material and the added "puff" given by way of this catalog serving as a sales vehicle.

A more-accurate and extensive study is d'Alte Welch's *A Bibliography of American Children's Books Printed Prior to 1821* (produced for, and published by, the American Antiquarian Society, 1972). Welch records and describes nearly 13,000 different printings of approximately 1,500 titles (as compared with Rosenbach's total listing of 596 items published before 1821). Welch cites institutional locations and occasionally comments on rarity, which is often implied from the number of known copies located by him and by details of any defects in those copies. A preliminary draft of this census, serialized from 1963 to 1967 in the *AAS Proceedings,* also details copies owned by private collectors. The details provided in the serializations were deleted when the Welch bibliography was published as a book. With all of these kudos, readers must be aware that even this bibliography has its own restrictions by excluding school texts, courtesy books, and religious instruction for children (all of which *are* included by Rosenbach).

These two references have been cited in particular detail to better explain how important source material may be restrictive despite its being authoritative. Both Rosenbach and Welch are excellent books when used within the context of their intended focus, but always be aware of such focus before you indicate a book's rarity by its absence from those sources. Aside from those "remainder" titles culled from Uncle Moses' trunk, it is rarer to find particular volumes that *are* described by Rosenbach (which is really a selective private collection) than it is to find something *not* in Welch that should otherwise be listed. In the quarter-century since Welch was last published, several hundred additional entries could be added—including some new titles (though mostly these would be hitherto unrecorded printings of book titles previously cited in other editions or previously known only from advertisements). For other references covering early American children's books, consult G. Thomas Tanselle's *Guide to the Study of United States Imprints.*

Using Collections Catalogs

Researchers and collectors should also consult published catalogs of both private and institutional collections of children's books along with important exhibition catalogs since these can be useful in helping to determine the publishing history of a particular text, the number of illustrations required for completeness, and general information about the author or the work itself. Such background data can help ascertain the value of individual titles.

The catalog of the Osborne Collection, at Toronto Public Library, volume 1, contains a valuable appendix that records early British publishers, booksellers, and printers involved in the production of children's books. The information assembled dates from 1958 when volume 1 was published, recording some 4,000 volumes held by the Osborne Collection at the time. Nearly four decades later the collection is six times the size it was in 1958. It is often incorrect to describe an item as "not in Osborne" simply because it isn't listed in the published Osborne Collection catalog (volume 2 of which appeared in 1975) unless the researcher has verified that the item truly is not in the collection. Be certain to remember the Osborne Collection's requisite focus is primarily on books published in Britain no later than 1910 (when Edgar Osborne determined he had outgrown his childhood library).

The Catalogue of Printed Books at the British Museum (acquired prior to 1955) as well as the *National Union Catalog* (compiled by the Library of Congress listing all books in American research collections published up to 1955) are excessively valuable references since they will often include dates for undated imprints and provide a useful cumulative listing of most known editions for any English language author or even book title. Appended to this chapter is a selected list of more-specific references, which can be enlarged upon by consulting Virginia Haviland's three-volume *Children's Literature: A Guide to Reference Sources.*

Using Internet Resources

The Internet is a unique research vehicle that allows you to verify the completeness and relative rarity of other copies of the same book or anything else you want to identify (though its search engines have so far tapped only surface dust from a great potential universe). While it is generally impossible for most collections to do 100 percent retrospective cataloging online to include all books previously described on old-fashioned index cards, since the 1970s (and perhaps earlier) library systems have been converting their latest records into database files that can be accessed by terminals all over the world via an electronic modem and a telnet address linking to a specific database.

The easiest access systems that currently allow free entry include MELVYL (University of California Libraries) and MaRK. MELVYL has nearly 9 million titles and almost 14 million holdings among its various campuses; it details books, serials, phonograph records, etc. MaRK represents the American Antiquarian Society's files for books, serials, manuscripts, and engravings (all American, from the beginning up to 1876). It can be searched using a combination of thirty-three indexes, including illustrator/engraver and former owner/donor besides the usual author, title, place of publication, publisher/printer, date, bibliographical citation, language, and so forth.

Several subscription databases exist for a fee of approximately $1 (plus/minus) per search. These include RLIN (Research Libraries Information Network) and OCLC (Online Computer Library Center), both of which provide information on U.S. research collections as well as public library systems throughout America. BLAISE is the online database for The British Library's relatively complete holdings. All three of these databases likewise include links to searching the ESTC (English Short Title Catalog for all books printed in that language pre-1801 regardless of where the printing was done).

Using Booksellers' Catalogs

Booksellers' catalogs are only as helpful in determining value as is the individual bookseller's level of expertise. Once books leave the bindery, no two copies are ever going to be identical in every respect, so the value determined by one bookseller for a particular work is not necessarily the same value that would be ascribed to another copy of that same edition. However, patterns do emerge, and over a period of time you can estimate current value by tracking past performance in the various catalogs of different dealers or auction galleries. As there is no licensing agency involved in qualifying anyone to become a bookseller or restricting the issuance of catalogs, you will also need to estimate the knowledge of those responsible for the descriptions and pricing to be able to judge accuracy. Perhaps it sounds naive, but just because someone calls a book a first edition, it doesn't mean that it is a first edition; bibliographic citations should confirm these details.

In our modern society filled with opportunities, we have occasionally lost sight of the responsibility that should exist between dealer and client where anyone interested enough to purchase a book should be able to ask all relevant questions as to the publishing history, bibliography, and even contents of a particular volume being offered for sale. It is the bookseller's requisite to be able to answer these questions correctly. That is what ultimately distinguishes a professional dealer from an amateur; there is a place for both to coexist, but the amateur should not try to imitate the professional. Some dealers have learned their trade through buying and selling old books at antique shows, and they have no concept of the internal makeup of a book or manuscript: They do not bother (or perhaps even know how) to collate, and they assume every volume they sell is complete by virtue of ownership. They call all books first editions unless the title page indicates otherwise. These may sound like extreme circumstances, but regretfully they are not. Clearly collectors cannot trust descriptions in catalogs issued by such people or judge the fairness of a book's price in this context. Such dealers are in the minority, but now they have become members of national trade associations and exhibit at book fairs, so be cautious.

Dealers' Experience

As alluded to in the introduction, about thirty years ago, I visited a specialist dealer in old children's books and happened to notice in his back room, alongside a packing table, a half-dozen books illustrated by Arthur Rackham that were falling apart out of their bindings. At that time Rackham books were collectible but not necessarily expensive, and copies such as these would be virtually worthless. I asked out of curiosity why he had such dreadful copies of books in his shop, and the dealer replied quite honestly that he used them to substitute damaged and missing color plates from other books he might get for inventory. I looked puzzled again, since the chances of replacing such defects with the same illustration seemed rather remote from this motley group of disbound rubble. He winked his eye, and explained further: very few buyers of Rackham books (he claimed) ever bother reading the texts, since they want the books just for the illustrations. So regardless of what plates he specifically needs, he replaces them with whatever is available, and no one knows the difference. I was shocked, and ever since then I have shuddered when I think of the number of mismatched and defective Rackham color-plate books that may have come onto the rare books market undetected. Who would ever know? The dealer was quite correct in his assumption, but it becomes a great moral and ethical issue . . . and should be a warning for everyone to carefully examine each book if only to prevent being caught by some nightmarish experience because something is wrong with an internal collation.

Know as much as you can manage about the books you want to have appraised; that is a safe way of testing the expertise of a dealer and likewise estimating his or her competence. Read everybody's catalog and through trial and error you will build up confidence with individual booksellers. You may find that a full-time specialist in children's books will charge a bit more for particular books, but there is the assurance that you are getting exactly what you believe you are purchasing, and in the long term the quality of material being sold by such people will prove the best value of all. In some cases, I have known a general dealer to price certain children's books higher than we do in our shop because the work looks more unusual to them or perhaps seems a bit more special; such are the vagaries of the trade.

Using Price Guides

In recent years there have appeared several other resources that might be called price guides, cumulative listings from the inventories of booksellers, in most cases culled from a selected group of antiquarian catalogs. The oldest of these is *Bookman's Price Index,* which is published twice annually and includes about 25,000 entries from nearly 200 booksellers in the United States, Britain, and Canada. It lists many genres beginning at about $100 value. Children's books are just one small part of this great chain. More specifically, Michael Cole began issuing a few years ago his *Annual Register of Book Values* with an entire volume devoted specifically to children's books from the eighteenth century to the present.

Then there is Interloc, an online service, which can connect you to an online database to search more than 1.6 million books for sale, or you can use its CD-ROM disc to check out nearly 400,000 book titles with values for items that have already been sold over Interloc. Therefore, these are not simply dealer asking prices but actually established sale prices. As mentioned previously, the problem always comes back to the level of expertise of both the buyer and the seller: A buyer can overpay substantially if offered a scarce book title without any point of reference. Likewise, a dealer may price some book outside his or her areas of special focus and just as easily grossly undervalue an item that sells quickly. Thus the price gets entered onto this price guide as an accurate selling value even though a much higher price could have been achieved with a bit more expertise.

Auctions

Auctions devoted entirely to children's books and related artwork have been held by Sotheby's (London) at least twice a year since 1967 and about twice a year at Christie's South Kensington (London); similar auctions are held less regularly in Germany, France, the Netherlands, and the United States. The accuracy of using these results as a guide for appraisals is subject to an improbable balance of factors—not to mention the talents of the cataloger in pointing out significant aspects of each item being offered. Perhaps the most accurate guide is not to judge the price certain books fetch but rather the frequency with which these titles come up for sale: one copy every year or two as compared to many copies being auctioned within the same year. As to value, all that an auction actually tells us is the top price an individual was willing to pay against competition assembled together in the same room on a particular day with the limited knowledge available to them. More times than one might realize, rare books are not always accurately identified by auction house descriptions, nor is condition necessarily sufficiently detailed when these records become abridged into cumulative price indexes. Too many amateurs rely on this form of misinformation to evaluate or consider book purchases, but in truth it is only one piece of an otherwise complex jigsaw.

A final remark regarding auction prices: when using them as a price guide, many books do form a pattern of values spanning a period of time. Always keep in mind, however, the fluctuating foreign exchange rates. In 1965 the British pound was worth $2.80; three years later, it was revalued to $2.40; and since then the currency market has been floating with the pound as low as $1.03 in 1983! Currently, it has been edging around the $1.60 mark, plus or minus. You can see the obvious difficulty in looking up auction prices in British pounds and not knowing the then current exchange against the U.S. dollar. Also note that the absence of any particular book in auction records does not mean that no other copies exist or that the book is so rare it is never offered for sale. It could mean that a specific title simply has not been sold at auction, or if it were sold at auction, perhaps it was lotted together with other volumes, which would prevent it from having a separate entry. On the other hand, it may have been considered too common a work to be assigned an auctionable value.

In summary, book appraisal is an individualized, subjective attitude toward fair-market value. It defies any set formula and requires a thorough knowledge of the field to place particular books into a historical perspective. Appraisers must be able to evaluate physical condition, verify completeness, correctly identify the printing history, assess relative rarity, and know the current price range for similar material. Doing appraisals is highly technical; it requires a great deal of experience and expertise. There are no shortcuts. I wish there were!

Further Reading

General Studies

Alderson, Brian. *Sing a Song for Sixpence: The English Picture Book Tradition and Randolph Caldecott.* Cambridge, Eng.: Cambridge Univ. Pr., 1986.

Andeas, Gesiena. *The Dawn of Literature in England.* Amsterdam: J. H. Paris, 1925.

Aries, Phillipe. *Centuries of Childhood.* New York: Knopf, 1962.

Barr, John. *Illustrated Children's Books.* London: The British Library, 1986.

Briggs, Katherine M. *The Fairies in Tradition and Literature.* London: Routledge & Kegan Paul, 1967.

Bruggemann, Theodor. *Handbuch zur Kinder- und Jugendliteratur von 1750 bis 1800.* Stuttgart: J. B. Metzler, 1982.

Caradec, Francois. *Histoire de la Litterature Enfantine en France.* Paris: Albin Michel, 1977.

Carpenter, Charles. *History of American Schoolbooks.* Philadelphia: Univ. of Pa. Pr., 1963.

Children's Books History Society. *The Cataloguing of Early Children's Books: A Guide for Collectors.* New Barnet, Herts, Eng.: CBHS, 1979.

"Children's Literature Collections and Research Libraries." *Wilson Library Bulletin* 50 (Oct. 1975).

Darling, Richard L. *The Rise of Children's Book Reviewing in America, 1865–1881.* New York and London: R. R. Bowker, 1967.

Darton, F. J. Harvey. *Children's Books in England.* Cambridge, Eng.: Cambridge Univ. Pr., 1932; 3d ed., rev. and ed. by Brian Alderson, idem, 1982.

Doderer, Klaus. *Lexikon der Kinder- und Jugendliteratur.* Weinheim and Basel, Switz.: Beltz, 1973–1982.

Egoff, Sheila. *The Republic of Childhood: A Critical Guide to Canadian Children's Literature in English.* Toronto: Oxford Univ. Pr., 1967.

Halsey, Rosalie V. *Forgotten Books of the American Nursery.* Boston: Goodspeed, 1911.

Hawkes, Louise R. *Before and After Pinocchio: A Study of Italian Children's Books.* Paris: Puppet Pr., 1933.

Hobrecker, Karl. *Alte Vergessene Kinderbucher.* Berlin: Mauritius, 1924.

Hurlimann, Bettina. *Three Centuries of Children's Books in Europe.* London: Oxford Univ. Pr., 1967.

Jackson, Mary V. *Engines of Instruction, Mischief, and Magic: Children's Literature in England from Its Beginnings to 1839.* Lincoln: Univ. of Nebr. Pr., 1989.

James, Philip. *Children's Books of Yesterday.* London: The Studio, 1933.

Kiefer, Monica. *American Children through Their Books.* Philadelphia: Univ. of Pa. Pr., 1948.

Mahoney, Bertha E., and Elinor Whitney. *Contemporary Illustrators of Children's Books.* Boston: Bookshop for Boys and Girls, 1930.

Mahoney, Bertha E., Louise P. Latimer, and Beulah Folmsbee. *Illustrators of Children's Books 1744–1945.* Boston: The Horn Book, 1947.

Meigs, Cornelia. *A Critical History of Children's Literature.* New York: Macmillan, 1953.

Muir, Percy H. *English Children's Books 1600 to 1900.* London: Batsford, 1954.

Phaedrus: An International Journal of Children's Literature. Edited by James H. Fraser, 1974–1980; retitled *Phaedrus: An International Annual for the History of Children's and Youth Literature.* Edited by James H. Fraser and Renate Raecke-Hauswedell, 1981–1988.

Pickering, Samuel F., Jr. *John Locke and Children's Books in Eighteenth-Century England.* Knoxville: Univ. of Tenn. Pr., 1981.

Pinchbeck, Ivy, and Margaret Hewett. *Children in English Society.* 2 vols. London: Routledge & Kegan Paul, 1969–1973.

Shepard, Leslie. *The History of Street Literature.* Detroit: Singing Tree, 1973.

Sloane, William. *Children's Books in England & America in the Seventeenth Century.* New York: King's Crown Pr., Columbia Univ., 1955.

Smith, Elva S. *The History of Children's Literature.* Chicago, 1937; revised and enlarged edition by Margaret Hodges and Susan Steinfirst. Chicago: American Library Association, 1980.

Summerfield, Geoffrey. *Fantasy & Reason: Children's Literature in the Eighteenth Century.* Athens: Univ. of Ga. Pr., 1985.

Tanselle, G. Thomas. *Guide to the Study of United States Imprints.* Cambridge, Mass.: Belknap Press of Harvard Univ. Pr., 1971.

Targ, William, ed. *Bibliophile in the Nursery: A Bookman's Treasury of Collector's Lore on Old and Rare Children's Books.* Cleveland: World, 1957.

Thwaite, Mary F. *From Primer to Pleasure in Reading.* Boston: The Horn Book, 1972.

Whalley, Joyce Irene. *Cobwebs to Catch Flies: Illustrated Books for the Nursery and Schoolroom 1700–1900.* London: Elek Books, 1974.

General Bibliographies

Adomeit, Ruth Elizabeth. *Three Centuries of Thumb Bibles: A Checklist.* New York: Garland, 1980.

Amtmann, Bernard. *Early Canadian Children's Books 1763–1840.* Montreal: Amtmann, 1976.

———. *A Bibliography of Canadian Children's Books 1841–1867.* Montreal: Amtmann, 1977.

Baker, Charles. *Bibliography of British Book Illustrators 1860–1900.* Birmingham, Eng.: Birmingham Bookshop, 1978.

Beall, Karen. *Cries and Itinerant Trades: A Bibliography.* Hamburg: Hauswedell, 1975.

Blanck, Jacob. *Peter Parley to Penrod: A Bibliographical Description of the Best-Loved American Juvenile Books.* New York: R. R. Bowker, 1938; revised 1956.

Commire, Anne, ed. *Something about the Author: Facts and Pictures about Authors and Illustrators of Books for Young People.* Detroit: Gale, 1971– .

Jones, Dolores Blythe. *Children's Literature Awards and Winners.* 3d ed. Detroit: Gale, 1994.

———. *Special Collections in Children's Literature: An International Directory.* 3d ed. Chicago: American Library Association, 1995.

Haviland, Virginia. *Children's Literature: A Guide to Reference Sources.* Washington, D.C.: Library of Congress, 1966; first supplement, 1972; second supplement, 1977.

Moon, Marjorie. *John Harris's Books for Youth 1801–1843.* Cambridge, Eng.: M. Moon, sold by A. Spilman, 1976. Supplement, Winchester, Eng.: M. Moon, sold by Five Owls Pr., 1983.

———. *Benjamin Tabart's Juvenile Library.* Winchester, Eng.: St. Paul's Bibliographies, 1990.

Muir, Marcie. *A Bibliography of Australian Children's Books.* 2 vols. London: Andre Deutsch, 1970–1976.

Nakamura, Joyce. *Children's Authors and Illustrators: An Index to Biographical Dictionaries.* 5th ed. Detroit: Gale, 1995.

Opie, Iona, and Peter Opie. *The Classic Fairy Tales.* London, Eng.: Oxford Univ. Pr., 1974.

———. *The Oxford Dictionary of Nursery Rhymes.* Oxford, Eng.: Clarendon Pr., 1951; repr. (with corrections), 1973.

Roscoe, Sydney. *John Newbery and His Successors 1740–1814.* Wormley, Eng.: Five Owls Pr., 1973.

Rumann, Arthur. *Alte Deutsche Kinderbucher.* Vienna: Reichner, 1937.

Wegehaupt, Heinz. *Alte Deutsche Kinderbucher 1507–1850, 1851–1900.* Hamburg: Hauswedell, 1979–1985.

Welch, d'Alte A. *A Bibliography of American Children's Books Printed Prior to 1821.* Worcester, Mass.: American Antiquarian Society, 1972.

Descriptive Catalogs of Collections and Exhibitions

Baldwin, Ruth. *Catalogue of the Baldwin Library of the University of Florida at Gainesville: An Index to Children's Books in English before 1900.* 3 vols. Boston: G. K. Hall, 1981.

Die Bilderwelt im Kinderbuch: Kinder- und Jugendbucher aus funf Jahrhunderten. Cologne: Kunst- und Museumbibliothek und Rheinisches Bildarchiv der Stadt Köln, 1988.

[Cahoon, Herbert]. *Children's Literature: Books and Manuscripts: An Exhibition.* New York: The Pierpont Morgan Library, 1954.

David, Linda. *Children's Books Published by William Darton and His Sons.* Bloomington: The Lilly Library, Ind. Univ., 1992.

Dusterdieck, Peter, comp. *Hobrecker: Die Sammlung Hobrecker der Universitatsbibliothek Braunschweig: Katalog der Kinder- und Jugendliteratur 1565–1945.* 2 vols. Munich: K. G. Saur, 1985.

Fieler, Frank B. *The David McCandless McKell Collection: A Descriptive Catalogue of Manuscripts, Early Printed Books, and Children's Books.* Boston: G. K. Hall, 1973.

[Gottlieb, Gerald]. *Early Children's Books and Their Illustration.* New York: The Pierpont Morgan Library, 1975.

Gumuchian & Cie. *Les Livres de l'Enfance du XVe au XIXe Siècle.* 2 vols. Paris: Gumuchian [1930].

Hamilton, Sinclair. *Early American Book Illustrators and Wood Engravers 1670–1870.* 2 vols. Princeton, N.J.: Princeton Univ. Pr., 1958–1968.

Hauswedell & Nolte. *Alte Deutsche Kinderbucher: Auktion # 200.* Hamburg: Hauswedell, 1974.

Moon, Marjorie. *The Marjorie Moon Collection of Early English Children's Books.* London: Christie's, 28 June 1995. Sale 5453.

[Muir, Percy H]. *Children's Books of Yesterday: Catalogue of an Exhibition.* London: National Book League, 1946; repr. with an index, Detroit: Singing Tree, 1970.

Opie, Iona, and Peter Opie. *Three Centuries of Nursery Rhymes and Poetry for Children.* London: Oxford Univ. Pr., 1973; 2d ed., enl. and indexed, 1977.

Rosenbach, A. S. W. *Early American Children's Books.* Portland, Maine: Southworth Pr., 1933.

St. John, Judith. *The Osborne Collection of Children's Books.* 2 vols. Toronto: Toronto Public Library, 1958–1975.

Schatzki, Walter. *Children's Books: Old and Rare.* Catalog No. One. New York: Walter Schatzki, bookseller, 1941; repr., Detroit: Gale, 1974.

Schiller, Justin G., Ltd. *Children's Books from Four Centuries.* Catalogue 29. New York: Schiller, 1973.

———. *Realms of Childhood.* Catalogue 41. New York: Schiller, 1983.

Seebass, Adolf. *Alte Kinderbuecher und Jugendschriften.* Katalog 636, 818. Basel, Switz.: Haus der Bucher, 1954–1983.

Shaw, John MacKay. *Childhood in Poetry: A Catalogue, with Biographical and Critical Annotations.* 10 vols. Detroit: Gale, 1968–1976.

Shirley, Betsy Beinecke. *A Child's Garden of Dreams: Children's Books and Their Original Illustration.* Chadds Ford, Pa.: Brandywine River Museum, 1989.

―――. *Read Me a Story—Show Me a Book: American Children's Literature 1690–1988.* New Haven: Yale Univ., 1991.

Sotheby & Co. *Catalogue of a Highly Important Collection of Children's Books in Seven Parts.* London: Sotheby, 1974–1982.

Spielmann, Percy Edwin. *Catalogue of the Library of Miniature Books.* London: Edward Arnold, 1961.

Swann Galleries, Inc. *Children's Books: Auction 1053.* New York: Swann, Feb. 1977.

Price Guides

Bookman's Price Index. Detroit: Gale Research, 1964– .

Cole, Michael. *Register of Book Values.* York, Eng.: The Clique, 1994.

Cataloging for Special Collections

Dolores Blythe Jones

Cataloging is the process that establishes bibliographic control over distinct items in a collection of books or other materials. A catalog can be as simple as an alphabetical title listing of all items in the collection. But, more likely, a library or collector will find an expanded catalog providing numerous access points to be more useful. Detailed cataloging often reveals hidden facts and relationships that were unknown when the books were grouped on the shelf by author, subject, or title. A well-organized catalog provides immediate knowledge of all aspects of a collection's holdings.

For the purposes of this chapter, the generic term *book* is used to describe monographs, audiovisual materials, microformats, and serial publications. The arrangement, description, and cataloging of primary source materials such as manuscripts, illustrations, correspondence, and other related items are discussed in chapter 5.

Although the benefits of cataloging are numerous, it is too often a neglected procedure. Cataloging is not as glamorous or visible as fund-raising and public relations. Uncataloged books do not demand the immediate attention that is required for a patron with a reference request. Acquisition is often a more rapid process than cataloging. It is quite possible to spend less time acquiring a donation of five hundred books than is necessary to catalog even one of those books. Most institutions have ever-growing backlogs of previously purchased or donated materials that will never receive the priority of newly purchased items.

Books found in children's literature special collections present challenges and problems that are unique to this genre. When cataloging a collection with a subject specialization, it is advisable to highlight the details, attributes, and qualities that make those books special. Different books are important for different reasons. The importance of a book may be determined by author, illustrator, publisher, printer, publication date, subject, or genre. The book may also be important as an artifact that beautifully displays marbled end papers, leather boards, or woodcut illustrations.

The specific needs of scholars using children's books for research must be addressed in the cataloging process. A collection of children's books assembled for the purpose of serving the scholarly community must be cataloged quite differently from the same collection of books designed to serve the casual reader or a preschooler. It is important for the cataloger to be aware of the important aspects of each book and to highlight these in the descriptive cataloging.

Since the catalog entry is often a researcher's first point of contact with a collection, it is to everyone's advantage to provide as much specific information as possible. But, as we all know, ideals must be tempered with reality. Many variables, most out of our control, will have a significant impact upon the level at which any special collection can be cataloged. The interplay of funding, personnel, time, institutional policies, user needs, availability of equipment, and features of online systems will determine exactly what can be accomplished.

Each situation in which we are called upon to provide cataloging for a special collection of children's literature is unique. In one example, a small public library has just received a donation of 300 historical children's books lovingly collected over the past twenty years by a library trustee. In another case, the new curator of a special children's collection at a university library is confronted with an 8,000-volume backlog; important books, but never high enough on the list of priorities to be cataloged. Consider also the private collector who now has 50 alphabet books in her growing collection and is seeking a way to maintain order and avoid duplication in future purchases.

Cataloging Plan

Each of these individuals needs a well-conceived plan of action before embarking on a long-term project to catalog his or her treasures and make them accessible to others. Although cataloging is a process that can be updated and elaborated upon, somehow there is never time to retrace our steps and correct yesterday's problems. Therefore, it is better to start with procedures that address the needs of the collection today as well as anticipate tomorrow's needs. As previously mentioned, this plan must take into account the policies and procedures of the institution or individual as well as reflecting the personnel, equipment, time, and funding available for the project.

This chapter does not provide a quick course in cataloging, nor does it provide a detailed step-by-step list of rules and standards. It is assumed that the reader has basic cataloging expertise that has been acquired through course work or on-the-job training. However, this chapter does provide suggestions and guidance for recording the information that can be included in the record.

Basics

The following discussion is based on the guidelines set forth in the *Anglo-American Cataloguing Rules* 2d ed., 1988 revision (AACR2). These guidelines are particularly pertinent for a collection consisting mainly of twentieth-century materials. For rare items, those printed in the eighteenth century or earlier, it is advisable to supplement the AACR2 guidelines with those set forth in *Descriptive Cataloging of Rare Books* 2d ed. (DCRB). DCRB is a cataloging standard, based on AACR2, that provides for a more-thorough and specialized treatment for rare books. As you may have noticed, nineteenth-century imprints are not precisely addressed by either code. The general practice of many special collections catalogers has been to use a locally formulated hybrid of AACR2 and DCRB for these items. Nineteenth-century imprints often have special features more common to earlier imprints, such as publishers, printers, and bindings, that need to be brought to the attention of researchers. Such special attributes can be highlighted through the combined use of AACR2 and DCRB codes.

The cataloging of any item begins with a determination of basic information such as author(s), illustrator(s), title, place and date of publication, publisher, edition, pagination, type of illustrations, and size. Additionally, special features are addressed revealing the more-detailed nature of the item. Examples of these special features include the recording of personal inscriptions; description of decorative bindings; creation of access points for the printer, publisher, engraver, and illustrator; recording of series title; notation of publisher advertisements and catalogs; description of signature notes; and citation of bibliographic references. Please remember, these features are only listed as possibilities, not absolutes. Each cataloger will need to ascertain which points are pertinent to the mission of the collection and its users.

Catalog Elements

The following sections discuss the elements that are comprised in a complete catalog record. The field name appears in boldface with the corresponding MARC tag number in parentheses. Examples are provided to illustrate the use of each element.

Main Entry (Personal Name 100; Corporate Name 110)

Personal and corporate names conform to AACR2 and Library of Congress (LC) practice. In some cases, it is not enough to merely transcribe the name that appears on the title page. Whatever form of the name is chosen, consistency is of ultimate importance.

Example

The title pages of three separate items read Theo Le Sieg, Theodor Geisel, and Dr. Seuss. Current practice favors the use of Dr. Seuss as the main entry for all three items. Cross references should be made from the other two names.

Uniform Title (130 or 240)

Uniformity is important for classic stories such as "Cinderella," "Little Red Riding Hood," and "Tom Thumb" that are published with a variety of titles. Use of a uniform title pulls together all variant forms.

Example

"Cinderella" is the uniform title chosen for *Cinderella and the Glass Slipper, The History of Cinderella,* and *My Book of Cinderella.*

Title Statement (245)

Transcribe the exact and complete wording and spelling as found on the title page, or cover if a title page does not exist. In many seventeenth- through nineteenth-century works issued in numerous editions, there are often subtle wording changes in the remainder of the title. It is important to record the entire title to ascertain these differences.

Example

The primer: set fvrth by the kinges maiestie & his clergie, to be taught, lerued, and red; & none other to be vsed thorowout all his dominions.

Edition Statement (250)

Indicate any edition information with corporate or personal responsibility that applies to that particular edition.

Example

Fourteenth edition, carefully revised and corrected throughout by Arthur Aikin.

Imprint (260)

Record the place of publication, publisher's name and address, and date of publication. It is important to include all cities and publishers with complete addresses. If printer information is given in the book, it can be added following the date.

Example

London : printed for Baldwin and Cradock; also for N. Hailes, Picadilly; and John Marshall, 1825 (London : T. C. Hansard, Pater-noster-row).

Physical Description (300)

Include pagination, illustrative matter, and dimensions. If a book measures less than 10 centimeters, the size is expressed in millimeters.

Example

24 p., [3] leaves of plates : ill. (some col.) ; 22 cm.

Series Statement (440 or 490)

Record the series title as it appears on the item being cataloged, including any volume or series numbering. This information can provide important links between titles in the same series.

Example

Little golden books 231

General Notes (500)

This field can contain general notes on information not given elsewhere in the record. Examples are signature statements, binding descriptions, presence of publisher catalogs, or advertisements.

Examples

Signatures: a^6, $B\text{-}R^6$.
Bound in blue morocco boards with gilt rule on cover.
Leaves top edges gilt, marbled end papers.
Publisher catalog on pp. 65-69.

Local Notes (590)

Information specific to the item in your collection can be included here. Inscriptions and imperfect-copy information are some examples.

Examples

Inscription reads "To Helen from Mother, Christmas 1823."
This library's copy lacking title page and pp. 12-16.

Contents (505)

If a volume contains several stories, it is often important to list these in a formatted contents note, thus allowing the item to be retrieved by the individual story titles, as well as the collective title.

Example

The emperor's new clothes - - The snow queen - - The ugly duckling - - The little mermaid.

Citation Note / References (510)

Standard bibliographic sources are often useful in verifying, identifying, and describing items. References to these standard bibliographic sources should be included in the cataloging record. Use *Standard Citation Forms for Published Bibliographies and Catalogs Used in Rare Book Cataloging* to ascertain the correct form of the citation.

Examples

References: Rosenbach, A.S.W. Children's books, 132.
References: Osborne Coll., p. 79.

Awards Note (586)

This field can be especially helpful in contemporary collections to identify titles that have won major awards in the field.

Example

Caldecott Medal, 1979.

Subject Entry (6XX)

Subject headings are often overlooked in cataloging children's literature, particularly for fiction titles. Since their approach is often topical, researchers find subject access to be particularly helpful.

Examples

African-Americans- -Juvenile fiction.
Child abuse- -Juvenile literature.
Counting- -Juvenile literature.

If the presence of a publisher's catalog is included in a general note, it should be given a subject heading.

Example

Catalogs, Publishers'- -John Newbery.

Genre Heading (655)

This heading is used to designate specific kinds of materials distinguished by the style or technique of their intellectual content (i.e., Alphabet books, Catechisms, Fairy tales, Juvenile literature, Hornbooks). It is possible to subdivide chronologically or geographically to provide more specific access.

Examples

Alphabet books- -1850.
Fairy tales- -France- -1710.

Added Entry (Personal Name 700)

Make entries for all joint authors, illustrators, engravers, and translators. Follow the same criteria as for Main Entry (100).

Added Entry (Corporate 710)

Make entries for all publishers and printers listed in the Imprint (260).

Examples

John Newbery- -publisher.
Sidney's Press- -printer.

Hierarchical Place Name Access (752)

Provides a hierarchical form of geographic access. This is used to indicate the place of publication.

Example

United States- -Connecticut- -New Haven.

Physical Characteristics Added Entry (755)

This entry allows for the description of physical aspects of the book such as paper, binding, typeface, graphic representations, and provenance. Although some of these same aspects can be covered in a 500 general note, the 755 field will more likely be a retrievable access point in many online catalogs, thereby allowing the information to be accessed in an automated search.

Examples

Dutch gilt papers.
Lithographs- -Germany- -1902.

Of course, there are other fields that can be used to provide information in the cataloging record. Those described here are the most commonly used and provide for the type of information needed by researchers and others accessing the catalog records.

Local Policies

To ensure uniformity from year to year and even day to day, maintain a policy manual or handbook that lists the policies and procedures that have been determined for your collection. Many children's books are undated, so you must establish a policy regarding how much information is needed before cataloging the item. AACR2 rules allow the cataloger to supply an approximate date as general as the probable century, that is, [18--] or [19--]. Some institutions, however, find this to be inadequate and do not catalog a book until a probable decade can be ascertained. In that case, the date on the catalog record would be listed as [185-] or [ca. 1855]. Probable dates can often be ascertained from inscription dates, bibliographies, and other reference sources.

You will need to make decisions regarding what information is necessary for a particular group of books. For example, you may find it worthwhile to have access points for publishers of books produced prior to 1900, but it may become too cumbersome after that date. Or you may wish to trace only those publishers who worked in certain cities or countries. A binding description may be pointless for a mundanely bound item, but highlighting a beautiful leather-bound volume decorated in gilt with marbled end papers may serve a purpose for your users. The same can also be said of routine inscriptions such as "To my favorite niece Mary from Aunt Martha, Christmas 1919." Unless the inscription provides information for an unknown publication date, it may be of little consequence. However, it is a different situation when the inscription reads "To Mary with love from Kate" and the "Kate" is Kate Greenaway.

In addition to the policy manual, it is helpful to have an authority file where the established names and dates for authors, illustrators, and translators used in the 100 and 700 fields can be recorded. This practice will prevent the possibility of separate entries under Lewis Carroll, Charles Lutwidge Dodgson, and C. L. Dodgson in the same catalog. A similar authority file can be devised for publisher and printer names that are listed in the 710 field. This publisher authority file provides cross references for individuals who worked with more than one firm during their careers and can also supply information on mergers and name changes. For example, the publisher authority file will alert you to the fact that there is a connection among the following firm names: Darton and Harvey; Darton, Harvey and Darton; Harvey and Darton; Harvey, Darton and Co.; Darton and Clark; William Darton; William Darton and Son; and William Darton, Jr.

Less-structured "working files" are also extremely helpful. As you catalog, you'll find that bits of information that were useful in solving one problem are pertinent to another title encountered five months later. Since it is impossible to keep numerous facts at your fingertips or to transfer knowledge from one cataloger to another, it is helpful to have these informal files to record the results of your research.

The way in which your catalog entry is recorded will be determined by the type of equipment made available for the project. Of course, catalog entries can be handwritten or typewritten, but most catalogers have access to a personal computer and printer. Use of a computer opens new worlds of bibliographic control. Numerous software programs are designed to assist with cataloging on a personal computer. It is pointless to go into detail about various programs here because rapid technological change will make many of today's popular programs outdated before this book is published.

Bibliographic Utilities

Most institutional cataloging departments take advantage of the shared cataloging provided through bibliographic utilities. Several international bibliographic utilities are headquartered in the United States, including OCLC, RLIN, and WLN. OCLC is the Online Computer Library Center located in Dublin, Ohio. RLIN, or Research Libraries Information Network, is a product of the Research Libraries Group headquartered at Stanford University. The smallest utility is the Western Library Network (WLN) in the state of Washington. Each utility has its own standards for data input, but all are MARC-based systems that accommodate the rules of AACR2 and DCRB. As with all computer technology, capabilities of these utilities advance rapidly as new hardware and software develop.

Internet Sources

The most exciting advancement in computer technology in recent years is the emergence of the Internet. Listservs, the World Wide Web, news groups, and E-mail link even the most isolated cataloger to a wide world of information and resources. A listserv discussion group of particular interest to catalogers is Autocat. The purpose of Autocat is to provide a forum for the discussion of matters of importance in library cataloging. To subscribe, send a message to

listserv@ubvm.cc.buffalo.edu/

A number of sources on the World Wide Web address the needs of catalogers. One outstanding source is the University of Michigan Original Cataloging page (http://www.lib.umich.edu/libhome/ocu/#top). Here you can find online cataloging tools such as country of publication and language codes, Library of Congress Cutter tables for assigning call numbers, links to LC Marvel, and OCLC Reference Sources for Cataloging. Also of interest are home pages for OCLC (http://www.oclc.org) and RLG (http://www-rlg.stanford.edu). These references merely scratch the surface of the electronic resources. A search of listservs, news groups, and Web sites will produce hundreds of interesting sites.

In this age of change there is at least one constant—the presence of materials that are rendered useless without the access provided by adequate cataloging. As caretakers of these treasures, the librarian, curator, and collector have the means by which to make the items accessible to all. Although the parameters for each individual cataloging record seem limitless at first, a quick study of the collection will reveal exactly what information needs to be provided to the user. The benefits of a well-organized and precisely cataloged collection will be as apparent and useful to the collection's owners and administrators as they are to the researchers.

Further Reading

Bibliographic Standards Committee of the Rare Books and Manuscripts Section (ACRL/ALA). *Genre Terms: A Thesaurus for Use in Rare Book and Special Collections Cataloguing.* 2d ed. Chicago: Assoc. of College and Research Libraries, 1991.

———. *Paper Terms: A Thesaurus for Use in Rare Book and Special Collections Cataloguing.* Chicago: Assoc. of College and Research Libraries, 1990.

———. *Type Evidence: A Thesaurus for Use in Rare Book and Special Collections Cataloguing.* Chicago: Assoc. of College and Research Libraries, 1990.

Descriptive Cataloging of Rare Books. 2d ed. Washington, D.C.: Cataloging Distribution Service, Library of Congress, 1991.

Gorman, Michael, and Paul W. Winkler. *Anglo-American Cataloguing Rules.* 2d ed., 1988 revision. Chicago: American Library Assoc., 1988.

Standards Committee of the Rare Books and Manuscripts Section (ACRL/ALA). *Binding Terms: A Thesaurus for Use in Rare Book and Special Collections Cataloguing.* Chicago: Assoc. of College and Research Libraries, 1988.

———. *Printing and Publishing Evidence: Thesauri for Use in Rare Book and Special Collections Cataloguing.* Chicago: Assoc. of College and Research Libraries, 1986.

———. *Provenance Evidence: Thesaurus for Use in Rare Book and Special Collections Cataloguing.* Chicago: Assoc. of College and Research Libraries, 1988.

Thesaurus for Graphic Materials. Washington, D.C.: Cataloging Distribution Service, Library of Congress, 1995.

Van Wingen, Peter, and Stephen Paul Davis. *Standard Citation Forms for Published Bibliographies and Catalogs Used in Rare Book Cataloging.* Washington, D.C.: Library of Congress, 1982.

5

Special Considerations of Original Materials

Dolores Blythe Jones and
Anne Lundin

Special collections of children's literature are often borne on the wings of original materials, which descend on a library and, in the flurry of their fall, call for decisions to be made for archives to arise. These original materials have an appeal as treasures for scholarly research as well as for educational use. Research collections of children's literature are unique in this dual approach—to children and young adults interested in how books are made and how authors and readers relate and to adult researchers studying the whole context of a literature for childhood as discrete texts.

Special collections of children's literature are found in a variety of institutions including college and university libraries, public libraries, research institutions, historical societies, and the homes of private collectors. This diverse body of caretakers brings varying levels of expertise and knowledge to their collections.

Topics covered in this chapter include the arrangement and description of original materials, storage considerations, and types of finding aids. A discussion of the international utilities, databases, electronic resources, and descriptive standards that help make these original materials accessible is also included. The chapter concludes with a list of helpful books and journal articles as well as organizations and archival suppliers.

The purpose of this chapter is not to present a processing manual but, instead, to provide a guide to the basic principles underlying the concepts of accessioning, arrangement, description, and access. It will lead the reader to the appropriate books, journals, manuals, and guides that *will* give step-by-step instructions. What is best for one institution may not necessarily work in another. Levels of staff, budget, and expertise will certainly affect the method used and the extent to which any particular collection is processed.

Definition of Original Materials

For the purposes of this chapter *original materials* are all items created in the process of book production, excluding the published book. Materials used in the creation of a children's book include preliminary notes, manuscripts, typescripts, galleys, and page proofs. In addition, an illustrated book may also have sketch books, sketches, studies, storyboards, dummies, color proofs, the finished artwork, paste-ups, and press sheets. Depending on the era in which the book was created and the technique used by the artist, there may be wood blocks, color separations, etching plates, or printing stones. The medium employed by the artist can include oil, acrylic, watercolor, crayon, marker, pen and ink, pastels, charcoal, and pencil.

Background research conducted by the author/illustrator might include magazine and newspaper articles, correspondence, photographs, slides, and notes on index cards. Items related to the publication of the book may include publisher correspondence, fan mail, reviews, royalty statements, promotional pieces, publicity articles, and copyright forms. Ephemeral items created by or related to the author/illustrator might include greeting cards, advertising cards, bookplates, posters, bookmarks, invitations, memorabilia, scrapbooks, paper dolls, dolls, photographs, slides, and toys.

Processing Guidelines

Processing has been described as "all steps taken in an archival repository to prepare documentary materials for access and reference use."[1] Processing involves many diverse activities, although all steps fall into one of three general categories—arrangement, conservation, and description. Conservation is addressed more fully in chapter 6; therefore, discussion in this chapter will concentrate primarily on arrangement and description.

The processing of original materials calls for the use of a unique scheme for intellectual control and access. The cataloging and classification standards used in traditional library-book processing are inappropriate for use with handwritten notebooks, galley sheets, typescripts, sketch books, oil paintings, realia, and the miscellaneous ephemera often found in special collections. These distinctive items require special handling by a staff sensitive to their particular needs.

Presently there are no guidelines that govern processing of the manuscripts and illustrations contained in special collections of children's literature. It has been necessary to borrow policies and procedures from the archival field and to modify its practices to suit the unique needs of children's literature special collections. Archival theory and practice have historically been concerned with the arrangement and description of organizational records and the personal papers of families and individuals, whereas the holdings of original materials in children's literature special collections consist primarily of literary manuscripts and illustrations.

After an initial survey of your library's holdings to determine possible interest and usefulness to researchers, you will need to organize the materials and make them accessible. Before embarking on an ambitious project to arrange and describe the unorganized piles of manuscripts, illustrations, personal papers, and other original materials acquired by your library over the past fifty years, it is wise to develop a processing manual. This manual should set forth policies, procedures, and guidelines as defined by your organization to provide guidance to your staff and become a basic reference tool for your everyday work. A processing manual gives step-by-step instructions, guaranteeing that all collections are processed following the same basic procedures. A good manual can be used by students, volunteers, and professionals alike, ensuring that the same procedures are used year after year.

Arrangement

Arrangement is defined in the Society of American Archivists glossary as "the process and results of organizing archives, records, and manuscripts in accordance with accepted archival principles, particularly provenance, at as many as necessary of the following levels: repository, record group or comparable control unit, sub-group(s), series, file unit, and document. The process usually includes packing, labeling, and shelving of archives, records, and manuscripts, and is intended to achieve physical or administrative control and basic identification of the holdings."[2]

The complexity of the arrangement process is primarily dependent upon the condition in which the materials arrive at your library. Some donors pack the materials neatly into boxes that have been carefully numbered and organized. Others seemingly open a file drawer and dump the contents into a cardboard box, hoping that the archivist will be able to make some sense from their disorganization. It is the archivist's job to place these materials into some logical order so bibliographic control can be established.

PROVENANCE AND ORIGINAL ORDER

When sorting and arranging the materials, you must take care to observe the principles of provenance and original order. *Provenance,* from the French, means "source or origin." In archival practice, adherence to the principle of provenance means that the records of a given creator must not be intermingled with those of another creator. That is, manuscript collections are never disassembled or interfiled; they are not regrouped and distributed into other chronological or subject files in the library.

The principle of original order states that "records [and papers] should be maintained in the order in which they were placed by the organization, individual, or family that created them."[3] This precept of original order does not have as much bearing upon the literary collections most commonly found in special collections of children's literature as it does on the more-traditional archival records and personal papers. Literary collections are best arranged by gathering all materials created and produced as a result of the publication of a particular work, be it a book, a speech, a magazine story, or a play. Materials pertaining to one particular title are often obtained by the collection in a piecemeal fashion—the manuscript and typescript in one donation, followed by the page proofs and galleys, and the reviews, publisher correspondence, and fan mail arriving in yet another donation. Although it is important to adhere to the aforementioned principles of provenance and original order, guidelines must also be established to process materials that are in no discernible order when transferred from the creator to the institution. The archivist must use an educated judgment to sort, arrange, and impose an order upon the materials that will facilitate research, always bearing in mind that history is created by the order imposed upon a collection.

ACCESSION SHEET

When materials are first given to or acquired by the library, an accession sheet, or inventory, is completed. This accession sheet lists

> the donor's name
> the date of the donation or purchase
> an accession number (such as 97-001, where *97* signifies the year 1997 and *001* refers to the first accession of that year)
> any legal terms governing the accession
> all materials received in a particular donation, including full bibliographic information for published items and a full description with number of pages or pieces for each item

When a collection is received by the institution, a case file is established for each donor. This case file contains all correspondence between the donor and the library as well as the accession sheets. Any other information gathered by the archival staff can be added to this file.

Before the materials can be arranged, it is essential to know as much as possible about their creator. It is imperative that the arranger consult standard biographical and bibliographical sources such as *Something about the Author,* the Junior Book of Authors series, and the Illustrators of Children's Books series. Try to obtain a complete bibliography of the works of the creator using these sources, along with a search of the OCLC or RLIN databases. The bibliography can be an important processing tool because the title used on preliminary manuscripts and typescripts is not always the title under which the work was published. The biographical information will also help determine the prominence of the individual and the time period in which he or she worked. If the author/illustrator is obscure, quite possibly the only information available may be contained in the collection itself.

Levels of Arrangement

There are five levels of arrangement generally accepted by curators and archivists alike. They are

1. repository
2. record group
3. series and subseries
4. file unit
5. document

Repository level arrangement refers to a division of the repository's entire holdings into several distinct groups. For example, in the Special Collections Department of the University of Southern Mississippi (repository), the de Grummond Children's Literature Collection holdings are separate from the historical manuscripts and political papers housed in the University Archives and Manuscripts.

Record groups are bodies of records related by creator, organization, or activity. For example, within the holdings of the de Grummond Collection, original materials created by James Marshall form a record group and are separated from the record group of materials created by Ezra Jack Keats.

Within the record group, *series and subseries* are the next subordinate bodies. *Series* are defined as "file units or documents arranged in accordance with a filing system or maintained as a unit because they relate to a particular subject or function, result from the same activity, have a particular form, or because of some other relationship arising out of their creation, receipt, or use."[4] Examples of series within the record group known as James Marshall Papers are "Correspondence," "Sketchbooks," "Books," "Magazines," "Cards," "Unidentified and Unpublished Books," and "Posters." Subseries within the "Books" series consist of original materials for individual book titles such as *The Adventures of Isabel, George and Martha,* and *The Stupids Die.*

The *file unit* is a collection of documents brought together for ease in filing. In our example of *The Adventures of Isabel,* file units consist of twenty-one pencil sketches, nine pen-and-ink sketches, a dummy, and twenty-one final illustrations.

The *document* is simply a single item within the file unit, for example, one of the twenty-one sketches.

The most important aspect of arrangement is the creation of an organizational scheme. The determination of how the papers should be grouped—the establishment of series—is of utmost importance because it is here that the character of the collection is expressed. As previously mentioned, the most logical arrangement for literary collections is the grouping together of all materials pertaining to a particular title. For example, in a different record group, the Ezra Jack Keats Papers, all materials related to the creation of *The Snowy Day,* regardless of format, are grouped together, as are those for *A Letter to Amy, Whistle for Willie,* and *Louie.* The subseries, *The Snowy Day,* contains a number of file units consisting of storyboards, dummies, manuscripts, typescripts, sketches, illustrations, proofs, collage fabrics, publisher correspondence, fan mail, and Caldecott Medal memorabilia. All materials pertaining to *A Letter to Amy, Whistle for Willie,* and *Louie* form their own subseries. If one distinct record group contains materials for forty different titles created by that one author/illustrator, there will be forty different subseries listed under the series "Books."

Many record groups will also contain materials that do not pertain to a particular book. These materials should be arranged in series that are most useful to researchers, such as general correspondence, personal papers, financial records, awards and commendations, photographs, and promotional materials.

Materials may require several sortings before all pertinent papers and documents are assigned to the appropriate series. At this point, do not take the time to do an item-by-item arrangement within each folder. Since there is still much interfiling and possible rearranging to do, it is best to use older, nonpermanent folders, each clearly labeled as to the contents. Once a final order has been established, the materials can be placed in permanent, acid-free folders that are labeled with complete information.

Conservation

Although preservation and conservation methods are covered in a separate chapter, a basic discussion of conservation procedures is also necessary in this context. Throughout the sorting process, you should employ basic conservation techniques to protect documents from deterioration and decay. Unfold and unroll all documents, although it may be necessary to humidify the items to accomplish this. If an item is too large to store in a flattened state, it is better to roll the item than to fold it. Remove letters from their envelopes and print any pertinent information from the envelope onto the letter, lightly with a number 1 pencil. Or, if you prefer, keep the envelope in a folder with the letter. Remove all staples, rubber bands, paper clips, pins, and other fasteners. Photocopy highly acidic items like newspaper clippings onto acid-free paper or deacidify the item. Remove dust and dirt on the surface of items with a soft cloth or brush. Mend torn items with Japanese rice paper. Never use adhesive tapes of any kind to mend tears.

After the record group has been sorted into series and subseries and arranged in a logical order and after the basic conservation measures have been taken, the materials are ready for final processing. Place documents into acid-free file folders large enough to completely cover them. Make a folder for items larger than the standard legal-sized file folder. Suppliers listed in an appendix at the end of this chapter can provide a heavy weight paper suitable for folders. Place small, easily misplaced items into an acid-free envelope before placing them in the folder.

Each folder should contain only related items. For example, a five-page manuscript, a fifteen-page dummy, and a ten-page typescript for *The Snowy Day* should be placed into three separate file folders. Five different versions of a typescript, each only four to five pages long, could be placed in the same folder, provided that they can remain separated. Split lengthier typescripts into more than one folder, divided into logical units such as chapters. In any case, each folder should not contain more than thirty to forty pages.

Label each folder with its contents. Necessary information includes the collection number, name of author/illustrator, series or subseries name, a brief description of contents, and box and folder number. For example, a folder within *The Snowy Day* subseries would read

DG0001   KEATS   THE SNOWY DAY   COLLAGE FABRICS   10/3

Write this information directly onto the file folder, and place the folders into acid-free boxes. Fill boxes with folders, but never too tightly. If a box is less than full, fill the excess space with pieces of acid-free corrugated cardboard. Attach self-adhesive labels to the outside of each box. Information on the box label should include record group number, record group name, box number, and an abbreviated contents list.

DG0001   EZRA JACK KEATS PAPERS   BOX 10   THE SNOWY DAY

Description

After the collection is accessioned, listed, sorted, arranged, foldered, labeled, and boxed, the descriptive phase of the processing procedure begins. *Description* is "the process of establishing intellectual control over holdings through the preparation of finding aids."[5] Finding aids can be grouped into three categories:

1. those created for internal control of collections/groups
2. those produced for in-house reference service
3. those published for out-of-house consumption

Finding aids produced for internal control are accession sheets and box inventories. As previously discussed, accession sheets, or inventory lists, are prepared when materials are first received by the library. Information includes the name of the donor, date of the contribution, accession number, legal terms governing the materials, and a complete list of all materials contributed. The box inventory is created after the arrangement phase once the materials are sorted, arranged, foldered, and boxed. This box inventory lists the contents of each folder within a particular box, giving data such as series, format, quantity, medium, dates, description of subject content, and relationship to other series.

Finding aids produced for in-house reference include registers, card catalogs, and online catalogs. These finding aids are designed to help the researcher understand the parameters of the collection and to locate needed information. A register describes the collection, giving provenance and conditions of administration. Scope and general content of the collection with inclusive dates are provided, as well as biographical information on the creator of the materials. An explanation of the arrangement is accompanied by listings of the individual box inventories. Size of the collection can be expressed in cubic feet, linear feet, or number of items.

Although the card catalog and online catalog are thought of primarily as listings of published books, they can be used effectively to alert researchers to the existence of original materials as well. Cataloging of original materials is discussed later in this chapter as it applies to the AMC Format, OCLC, and RLIN.

Accession sheets and box inventories enable the special collections staff to gain bibliographic control over the original materials in their holdings. Thanks to registers and card catalogs, a researcher who visits a collection can gain access to needed materials. The recent availability of online catalogs enables researchers to ascertain pertinent information about particular items in a library's holdings from any remote location.

Publicizing Collection Availability

But what of the person who doesn't even know where to begin looking for elusive original materials? How does someone in Massachusetts know what is in a library in California, or for that matter, how does a British scholar know of the contents of a special collection in Hattiesburg, Mississippi? There are established procedures to inform the scholars of the existence of materials germane to their research. Curators of special collections can place notices in scholarly journals, describing new acquisitions and giving specific information regarding their use. The same type of announcements can be placed on listservs, news groups, and Web sites. Presentations at regional, national, and international conferences can alert scholars to previously hidden resources. Collection descriptions can be included in the *National Union Catalog of Manuscript Collections* (NUCMC). Catalog records, using the Archival and Manuscripts Control Format (AMC) can be entered into the databases of OCLC (Online Computer Library Center) or Research Libraries Group (RLIN). (A more detailed discussion of AMC, OCLC, RLIN, and NUCMC follows.)

One of the best ways to notify scholars of the holdings of special collections is through a published guide that lists every collection or record group in the repository, giving details of its contents. The guide can be published and made available to scholars throughout the world. Guides are time consuming and can be expensive; therefore, very few special collections of children's literature are fortunate enough to have this access tool. In 1985 *The Kerlan Collection Manuscripts and Illustrations for Children's Books: A Checklist* was published. It commemorates 35 years of the Kerlan Collection, housed at the University of Minnesota, and indexes the manuscripts and illustrations of more than 4,950 book titles representing 640 authors and illustrators.

MARC AMC

A goal of most special collections is the ability to exchange information concerning their holdings with scholars and similar special collections throughout the world. To achieve this transference of data in the most efficient manner, it is best to use a standardized format that is known and understood the world over. Such a format is the USMARC Archival and Manuscripts Control Format (AMC).

AMC is one of a family of formats for *MA*chine *R*eadable *C*ataloging (MARC) that was developed by the Library of Congress. The formats are used in the automated bibliographic and administrative control of information about materials found in libraries, archives, and other research institutions. The AMC Format specifies the type of information to be included and how it is expressed and provides a means for identifying the data elements through the use of a labeling system of field and subfield tags, indicators, and special codes. The AMC Format is the standard used in creating data records for original materials and is the starting point for contributing information to international databases such as NUCMC, OCLC, and RLIN. An essential reference tool for anyone considering the use of the MARC AMC Format is *MARC for Archives and Manuscripts: The AMC Format* by Nancy Sahli.

Once a library has achieved bibliographic control over its materials on an in-house level, it is possible to provide the same information in a slightly modified form to an international audience.

OCLC and RLIN

Another way to achieve international dispersal of holdings information is to catalog the original materials using a regional or national online network such as OCLC or RLIN. Both OCLC and RLIN are MARC-based automated information systems that maintain extensive bibliographic databases for shared cataloging. OCLC practice is based on its publication *Bibliographic Formats and Standards*, while RLIN practice is based on *RLIN Supplement to USMARC Bibliographic Format*. Both of these standards are in turn based on the Library of Congress's *USMARC Format for Bibliographic Data*. *MARC for Archives and Manuscripts: A Compendium of Practice* by Max J. Evans and Lisa B. Weber is a good source that details how the MARC AMC Format is being interpreted and used by a variety of institutions including OCLC and RLIN.

Catalogers of original materials must know different formats and adhere to different rules than do book catalogers. Book catalogers will be familiar with the *Anglo-American Cataloguing Rules,* 2nd edition, 1988 revision (AACR2), the standard set of rules designed for use in the construction of library catalogs. The rules cover the description of and the provision of access points for all library materials commonly collected. When cataloging manuscript and illustrative materials, it is important to follow the rules set forth in chapter 4 of AACR2. Chapter 4 covers "the description of manuscript (including typescript) materials of all kinds, including manuscript books, dissertations, letters, speeches, etc., legal papers (including printed forms completed in manuscript), and collections of such manuscripts."[6] The application of these basic rules to modern manuscript collections is discussed in *Archives, Personal Papers, and Manuscripts: A Cataloging Manual for Archival Repositories, Historical Societies, and Manuscript Libraries* by Steven L. Hensen. This work provides rules, in much the same format as AACR2, intended for use in the construction of entries by institutions that want to provide archivally oriented cataloging for their original materials.

The National Union Catalog of Manuscript Collections (NUCMC) is an international finding aid, first published in 1959 by the Library of Congress. NUCMC provides descriptions of thousands of manuscript collections housed in repositories throughout the United States. Collections of less than fifty items are excluded. Volumes of NUCMC are produced annually and date back to 1959. Its bibliographic records are created in the RLIN database and tapes are subsequently loaded by OCLC. NUCMC is a product of the Special Materials Cataloging Division of the Library of Congress.

Armed with the proper books, guides, and manuals, most librarians, curators, and collectors will find that the management of original materials is not as difficult as first thought.

Notes

1. Maygene F. Daniels and Timothy Walch, *A Modern Archives Reader: Basic Readings on Archival Theory and Practice* (Washington, D.C.: National Archives and Records Service, U.S. General Services Administration, 1984), 341.

2. Frank B. Evans, "A Basic Glossary for Archivists, Manuscript Curators, and Records Managers," *The American Archivist* 37 (July 1974): 415–33.

3. Daniels and Walch, 341.

4. Evans, 430.

5. Evans, 421.

6. Michael Gorman and Paul W. Winkler, eds., *Anglo-American Cataloguing Rules,* 2d ed., 1988 revision (Chicago: American Library Assoc., 1988), 123.

Further Reading

Bellardo, Lewis, and Lynn Lady Bellardo. *A Glossary for Archivists, Manuscript Curators, and Records Managers.* Chicago: Society of American Archivists, 1992.

Bradsher, James Gregory, ed. *Managing Archives and Archival Institutions.* Chicago: Univ. of Chicago Pr., 1991.

Daniels, Maygene F., and Timothy Walch. *A Modern Archives Reader: Basic Readings on Archival Theory and Practice.* Washington, D.C.: National Archives and Records Service, U.S. General Services Admin., 1984.

Duckett, Kenneth W. *Modern Manuscripts: A Practical Manual for Their Management, Care, and Use.* Nashville, Tenn.: American Assoc. for State and Local History, 1975.

Ellis, Judith, ed. *Keeping Archives.* Port Melbourne, Aust.: D. W. Thorpe with the Australian Society of Archivists, 1993.

Evans, Linda J., and Maureen O'Brien Will. *MARC for Archival Visual Materials: A Compendium of Practice.* Chicago: Chicago Historical Society, 1988.

Evans, Max J., and Lisa B. Weber. *MARC for Archives and Manuscripts: A Compendium of Practice.* Madison: The State Historical Society of Wisconsin, 1985.

Gorman, Michael, and Paul Winkler, eds. *Anglo-American Cataloguing Rules.* 2d ed. 1988 revision. Chicago: American Library Assoc., 1988.

Hensen, Steven L. *Archives, Personal Papers, and Manuscripts: A Cataloging Manual for Archival Repositories, Historical Societies, and Manuscript Libraries.* 2d ed. Chicago: Society of American Archivists, 1989.

Hoyle, Karen Nelson. *The Kerlan Collection Manuscripts and Illustrations for Children's Books: A Checklist.* Minneapolis, Minn.: Kerlan Collection, Univ. of Minn. Libraries, 1985.

Library of Congress. *National Union Catalog of Manuscript Collections.* Washington, D.C.: Library of Congress, 1959– .

———. *USMARC Format for Bibliographic Data.* Washington, D.C.: Cataloging Distribution Service, Library of Congress, 1994– .

Matters, Marion. *Introduction to the USMARC Format for Archival and Manuscripts Control.* Chicago: Society of American Archivists, 1990.

Miller, Frederic M. *Arranging and Describing Archives and Manuscripts.* Archival Fundamentals Series. Chicago: Society of American Archivists, 1990.

OCLC Online Computer Library Center. *Bibliographic Formats and Standards.* 2d ed. Dublin, Ohio: OCLC, 1996.

Pugh, Mary Jo. *Providing Reference Services for Archives and Manuscripts.* Archival Fundamentals Series. Chicago: Society of American Archivists, 1992.

Research Libraries Information Network. *RLIN Supplement to USMARC Bibliographic Format.* Mountain View, Calif.: RLIN, 1989.

Sahli, Nancy. *MARC for Archives and Manuscripts: The AMC Format.* Chicago: Society of American Archivists, 1985.

Schellenberg, T. R. *Modern Archives: Principles and Techniques.* Chicago: Univ. of Chicago Pr., 1956.

Smiraglia, Richard P., ed. *Describing Archival Materials: The Use of MARC AMC Format.* Binghamton, N.Y.: Haworth, 1990.

Society of American Archivists, Forms Manual Task Force. *Archival Forms Manual.* Chicago: Society of American Archivists, 1982.

"Standards for Archival Description." *The American Archivist* 52 (fall 1989).

Thesaurus for Graphic Materials. Washington, D.C.: Cataloging Distribution Service, Library of Congress, 1995.

Walch, Victoria Irons. *Standards for Archival Description: A Handbook.* Chicago: Society of American Archivists, 1993.

APPENDIX A

Organizations

Association for Library Collections and Technical Services
American Library Association
50 E. Huron St.
Chicago, IL 60611
(800) 545-2433;
 (800) 545-2444 (Illinois)

Association for College and Research Libraries
Rare Books and Manuscripts Section
American Library Association
50 E. Huron St.
Chicago, IL 60611
(800) 545-2433; (800) 545-2444 (Illinois)
http://www.princeton.edu/~ferguson/rbms.html

National Information Standards Organization
National Institute for Science and Technology
Administration 101, RIC E-106
Gaithersburg, MD 20899
(301) 975-2814
http://www.suncompsvc.com/niso/maina.htm

National Archives and Records Administration
Publications Services Branch (NEPS)
Washington, DC 20408
(202) 501-5240
http://www.nara.gov

National Union Catalog of Manuscript Collections
Library of Congress
Special Materials Cataloging Division
LM 547
Washington, DC 20541
(202) 707-7954
Fax: (202) 707-7161
E-mail: NUMC@mail.loc.gov
http://lcweb.loc.gov/coll/nucmc/nucmc.html

OCLC Online Computer Library Center
6565 Frantz Rd.
Dublin, OH 43017-0702
(614) 764-6000
http://www.oclc.org

Research Libraries Information Network
Research Libraries Group, Inc.
1200 Villa St.
Mountain View, CA 94041-1100
(415) 962-9951
http://www.rlg.org

Society of American Archivists
600 S. Federal, Ste. 504
Chicago, IL 60605
(312) 922-0140
http://volvo.gslis.utexas.edu: 80/~us-saa/

APPENDIX B

Archival Materials Suppliers

Archivart Division
Heller & Usdan
7 Caesar Pl.
Moonachie, NJ 07074
(800) 804-8428
Fax: (201) 935-5964

Conservation Materials
240 Freeport Blvd.
P. O. Box 2884
Sparks, NV 89432
(702) 331-0582

Conservation Resources
   International, Inc.
8000-H Forbes Pl.
Springfield, VA 22151-2204
(800) 634-6932
Fax: (703) 321-0629
E-mail: CONSRESUSA@aol.com

Dick Blick Art Materials
P. O. Box 1267
Galesburg, IL 61401
(800) 447-8192 (orders);
   (800) 933-2542 (product
   information)
Fax: (800) 621-8293
E-mail: INSO@DICKBLICK.com

Gaylord Bros.
P. O. Box 4901
Syracuse, NY 13221-4901
(800) 448-6160
Fax: (800) 272-3412
http://www.gaylord.com

The Hollinger Corp.
P. O. Box 8360
Fredericksburg, VA 22404
(800) 634-0491
Fax: (800) 947-8814
E-mail: hollingercorp@inter-
   serf.net

Light Impressions
439 Monroe Ave.
P. O. Box 940
Rochester, NY 14603-0940
(800) 828-6216
Fax: (800) 828-5539

Pohlig Bros., Inc.
Century Archival Products
P. O. Box 8069
Richmond, VA 23223
(804) 644-7824

Talas
Technical Library Service
568 Broadway
New York, NY 10012
(212) 219-0770

University Products, Inc.
517 Main St.
P. O. Box 101
Holyoke, MA 01041-0101
(800) 628-1912; (800) 336-4847
   (Massachusetts)
Fax: (800) 522-9281

6

Preservation
and Security

Mary Bogan

Institutions with special collections have a moral responsibility to preserve them. Any institution that establishes a special collection must carefully evaluate the resources needed to preserve it. If an institution has a special collection it cannot afford to preserve, that institution should seriously consider finding another appropriate institution that has the necessary resources to provide a home for the collection. Institutions with special collections should be prepared to invest resources in appropriate staffing and housing to ensure that valuable materials will be available for present and future researchers and other qualified users.

Many librarians have become curators of special collections of children's literature without specialized training in the field of preservation. Such a librarian may be confronted with severe preservation problems, as I was after becoming the curator of the May Massee Collection, which honors the second editor of children's books in the United States. (May Massee established the first children's book departments at Doubleday, Page and Company in 1923 and at the Viking Press in 1933. The May Massee Collection contains the books that she published as well as manuscripts, original artwork, and other materials related to the publishing of those books.) I discovered that original acetate artwork in the collection, which had been used in the publication of some major twentieth-century American children's books, had seriously deteriorated. Through continuing education, research, reading, involvement in professional organizations, and the development of a network of knowledgeable colleagues, I became informed about basic preservation. So, too, can you.

With this knowledge you can learn how to cope with such problems and, more importantly, learn how to prevent them. You can also become informed about the work of professional conservators and the roles of the conservator and the librarian in preservation. Part of this knowledge should include an awareness of your and others' limitations in the area of preservation; only those with the appropriate level of experience should attempt to do conservation work that requires professional expertise.

Terminology

In *Conservation of Cultural Property in the United States: A Statement* (1976), the National Conservation Advisory Council defined conservation as including these specific roles: examination, preservation, and restoration.

> Examination involves determining the original state of an item, such as a book or manuscript, with regard to its structure and composition as well as the extent to which the item has deteriorated.
> Preservation involves activities that would slow down or prevent the item from deteriorating or being damaged.
> The environment in which the item is housed can be controlled or the structure and material can be treated to achieve this goal.
> Restoration is returning an item that has deteriorated or been damaged to its original state as closely as possible without compromising the integrity of the item.[1]

Confusion exists in the usage of terminology in this field. Paul Conway points out the necessity for standard definitions in preservation education for the terms *conservation* and *preservation* in his 1989 article, "Archival Preservation: Definitions for Improving Education and Training." Currently, the trend is to use the term *preservation* as the more general term. *Conservation* is currently used as the more-specific term referring to performing treatments on the materials.[2]

The Need for Preservation

Librarians care about the preservation of books, manuscripts, artwork, and other materials in special collections because they are concerned with the preservation of the ideas that are transmitted through these media. Society depends on the unbroken transmission of accumulated knowledge that links the past to the future in the field of children's literature as well as in other fields. A librarian with a background in preservation can be more responsible in providing the care that treasures in children's literature special collections deserve.

Preservation should be an integral part of the management of special collections. Preventative maintenance is crucial for the preservation of the materials in a special collection. The curator must make sound decisions on what he or she knows to be best for the collection weighed against the reality of the institutional environment that may not have the optimum conditions.

Damage to materials can be caused by acidity of the materials themselves or environmental factors such as heat, humidity, air pollution, light, people, and fungi as well as insects and rodents. The curator should be careful when solving one environmental problem not to create another. For example, the use of poison may exterminate insects or rodents, but the same poison may be dangerous not only to the materials in the collection but also, more importantly, to the people who work in the collection or use the materials in the collection.

Much of the preservation work that has to be accomplished in a library can be performed by the library staff. The following bears repeating: Preservation work that is beyond the expertise of the staff should be left to professional conservators.

Basic Principles of Conservation

Librarians should keep in mind certain basic principles of conservation as taught in preservation workshops sponsored by the Society of American Archivists and the American Association for State and Local History.

1. *Rule of Reversibility.* Don't undertake any treatment that cannot be undone. (For example, don't laminate materials in special collections. Do use encapsulation, which is a reversible process.)

2. *Compatibility of the Solution to the Problem.* Don't apply a solution that is stronger than the problem. (For example, don't use heavy repair tape on a fragile item. Use materials and colors to blend with the age of the materials being preserved.) Don't use a technology just because it exists. Every technology and procedure must be evaluated in terms of reversibility and a given situation.
3. *Restoration.* The stability of the item should be the primary concern. The integrity of the item should not be compromised.
4. *Documentation.* Keep a carefully written record of any conservation procedures.
5. *Evaluation.* Weigh the intrinsic value of the material against the cost of preservation. The curator may decide that it is best to do nothing if there is no appropriate method available or if an available method is too expensive. No treatment is better than the wrong treatment for a conservation problem.

Responsibilities of a Preservation Librarian

Library directors should be encouraged to appoint a preservation librarian and empower that person to implement changes. The preservation librarian should conduct ongoing training for staff members to create a preservation mentality. For example, the Association of Physical Plant Administrators and the Commission on Preservation and Access engaged in a joint task force and developed a preservation course for physical plant administrators who work with academic libraries.[3] Such a course could be adapted for similar personnel in other types of libraries.

The preservation librarian should also be responsible for formulating a disaster plan, with input from other members of the staff including the curator of special collections. In addition to such natural disasters as earthquakes, floods, tornadoes, hurricanes, and other severe storms, such a plan should include strategies for coping with fires, power outages, plumbing problems, and malfunctioning heating/cooling systems. A malfunctioning heating system may generate excessive heat and humidity. A leak in the air-conditioning system can emit dangerous gas. An extended power outage can result in the loss of heating or cooling as well as humidity control. Such conditions can be hazardous for the staff and public as well as being detrimental to the materials.

As mentioned in the basic principles of conservation, the preservation librarian or curator should also be involved in developing policies regarding the appropriate use of chemicals in the library for insect extermination or cleaning. Some chemicals used for cleaning can be hazardous to people as well as to the materials.

Security Issues

The preservation librarian and/or curator should confer with law enforcement officers and locksmiths about security measures, and if necessary, a security system should be installed. Security of the special collections must be ensured. The collections must be in locked cases or rooms with key access limited to appropriate staff. Windows should be secure, and there should be no unsecured entrances from tunnels, equipment rooms, or roofs.

References should be checked when hiring staff, including student assistants for special collections. Although it may not be possible to do a thorough security check before hiring staff members, a few phone calls to appropriate individuals can yield valuable information about the applicants. Phone calls to individuals who are not listed by the applicants as references can often provide information that would determine whether a person would be an appropriate staff member in special collections.

Staff should be educated regarding security precautions. The staff's attitude influences the public in the handling of materials in special collections.

Patrons using materials in special collections should be carefully monitored to prevent theft and damage to the materials. Coats, purses, briefcases, and other packages should be left in a secure area so that materials cannot be removed easily from the collections. No special privileges should be granted to individuals. A tactfully worded concise statement of policies regarding the use of special collections should be given to each user. Those using the collection should register and show identification. They should sign forms listing the materials that they intend to use.

Environmental Issues

The appropriate physical environment is essential to the preservation of materials in special collections. A policy prohibiting eating, drinking, smoking, and the chewing of tobacco or gum by the public and the staff should be posted prominently and enforced.

(Ideally, these activities should be prohibited in the library as a whole and not only in special collections.) Any area where these activities are allowed for the library staff should be as far away as possible from the special collections. The area should be frequently cleaned and trash disposed of promptly so insects and rodents do not become a problem.

Policies regarding the duplication of materials in special collections by photocopiers and photographic methods should be developed with regard to preservation of the materials and protection of copyright.

Those using materials in special collections should use pencils to prevent possible damage to the materials. Cotton gloves should be furnished to the staff and the public to handle fragile materials that are not in protective enclosures.

Precautions should be taken to protect exhibited materials from damage caused by light, heat, and humidity. The duration of an exhibit should not present preservation hazards to the materials. Appropriate cases and archival-quality supplies should be used to protect the materials.

The temperature and humidity should be maintained at stable levels and be monitored on a daily basis. Air quality is also a major concern. *Preserving Archives and Manuscripts* by Mary Lynn Ritzenthaler includes an excellent discussion on the appropriate environment for materials found in special collections and archives. The author also presents practical information about how to achieve such an environment.[4]

The placement of shelving and cases is critical; they should not be located near sources of heat such as radiators and steam pipes. Steel shelving with a baked enamel finish and adjustable shelves is preferred. Closed cases will provide protection from dust.

Storage

Bound volumes should be stored upright on clean, smooth shelving, with oversized volumes stored horizontally to prevent the book block and the binding from separating due to the force of gravity. Keep all volumes upright and firmly supported on each side. If a book leans for even a few weeks, a permanent deformity of the spine can develop. The stresses set up within the binding may tear it apart while it is on the shelf.

Books should not be forced onto crowded shelves. Covers can be abraded, and the additional pressure can crack a spine. They should be gently grasped in mid-spine for easy removal from the shelf. When a book is grasped at the headcap of the spine, a torn spine often results. If necessary, books on either side of the desired one may be gently pushed in, so that the appropriate book can be grasped more easily for removal.

Fragile books with loose bindings can be tied together with archival-quality flat string. Protective wrappers and boxes can be ordered from library and conservation suppliers (see appendix B of chapter 5) or custom made in most libraries. The design should be kept simple for easy removal, and the box should fit snugly, but not too tightly, to reduce unnecessary movement.

Processing

If a volume is rare or special, processing should be kept to a minimum. Markings should be done with a number 2 pencil, and no pressure-sensitive or heat-sensitive labels should be applied to the volume. The call number can be indicated on a buffered paper strip that is placed in the volume.

Educational Resources

The Society of American Archivists Basic Manual Series includes *Archives and Manuscripts: Administration of Photographic Collections* as well as *Archives and Manuscripts: Exhibits*.[5] These volumes contain lists of recommended supplies and equipment used in the preservation of various types of materials in special collections and archives as well as sources for these supplies and equipment. Appendixes to this chapter also provide sources of valuable information about preserving a wide spectrum of formats.

Librarians who are responsible for special collections can find a number of continuing-education resources to support their pursuit of knowledge in the field of preservation. Institutions concerned with preservation include schools of library and information management, the Library of Congress, the National Archives and Records Administration, libraries, archives, historical societies, art galleries, museums, conservation laboratories, and regional conservation centers. A number of these are listed in appendix B at the end of this chapter. Corporations that manufacture materials that need to be preserved, such as film, as well as those companies that manufacture or sell preservation supplies and equipment can also be sources of information.

Schools of library and information management are concerned with educating their students in preservation. These schools could also provide a valuable service to professional librarians and information managers by providing continuing education in the area of preservation. In 1989, the Association for Library and Information Science Education (ALISE) formed a special interest group concerned with preservation education.

The Task Force on Preservation Education of the Commission on Preservation and Access has issued *Preservation Education Institute Final Report* summarizing the sessions held at the institute from August 2 through August 4, 1990. These sessions included educators from schools of library and information management, administrators in the library field, preservationists, archivists, and others who discussed the possibility of preservation receiving more emphasis in the curricula of schools of library and information management.[6]

The Library of Congress and the National Archives and Records Administration are very active on the national level in the field of preservation. Both institutions have conservation laboratories staffed by professional conservators and both have sponsored conferences and symposia on various aspects of preservation. The National Archives and Records Administration also sponsors the biennial Modern Archives Institute, which includes a preservation component.

Academic libraries, special libraries, major public libraries, state historical societies, museums, and art galleries may also have preservation staff and programs, as well as conservation laboratories. Although these institutions may not have specific children's literature materials, they will have materials in the same formats as those found in children's literature special collections.

When attending professional conferences of library and archival associations, you will find tours of conservation laboratories to be valuable experiences. You can learn firsthand how the staff of these laboratories solve various conservation problems and seek advice on handling conservation problems encountered in your own collection. It is also an excellent way to make contact with librarians and other professionals in the conservation field with whom you can network regarding preservation policies and problems.

Regional conservation centers are nonprofit organizations established to conserve the resources found in collections in libraries, archives, art museums, and historical institutions. (See appendix B at the end of this chapter.) Membership is available to nonprofit institutions that have artwork or other culturally significant items in their collections. After paying an annual membership fee, members can contract for conservation services at an hourly rate. These conservation services may also be available to nonmember educational or charitable institutions at fees that are set by each conservation center. Services provided constitute a comprehensive conservation program. On-site surveys include an assessment of environmental and storage conditions as well as the assessment of the condition of individual items and their conservation needs. In addition to the nonprofit regional conservation centers, there are also private conservation labs, conservation guilds, associations, and centers that provide services on a profit-making basis.

Membership in professional organizations concerned with preservation is essential to the librarian who is responsible for the preservation of resources in children's literature special collections. Sections of the American Library Association that are specifically involved with preservation are the Preservation and Reformatting Section of the Association for Library Collections & Technical Services and the Rare Books and Manuscripts Section of the Association of College and Research Libraries. Of course, the Association of Library Services for Children, whose members created this handbook, is also concerned with this issue.

The Preservation Section of the Society of American Archivists is very active, as is the American Association for State and Local History. Both organizations conduct workshops and publishing programs.

Membership in state and regional library associations, archival associations, and historical associations can also be valuable for the librarian who is interested in preservation. Although archival associations are not organized on the state level, there are active groups in many urban areas that include members in adjacent states. Librarians, historians, and museum personnel may also be organized on a local basis.

Professional library, archival, historical, and museum organizations on the national, regional, and state levels often sponsor conferences, preconferences, or workshops that deal with preservation. Members of these professional organizations receive mailings that detail conferences, meetings, workshops, and publications. Such activities, workshops, and meetings can provide a librarian who is interested in preservation issues with valuable educational experiences, opportunities to visit institutions involved in preservation, and chances to make valuable personal contacts. Periodicals in the preservation field also contain information about conferences, meetings, and workshops.

Educational opportunities and workshops are available through state programs such as the New York State Program for the Conservation and Preservation of Library Resource Materials, through regional library networks such as the Southeastern Library Network (SOLINET), and through regional conservation centers such as the Northeast Document Conservation Center.

If courses, meetings, and workshops related to preservation issues are not available in your area, perhaps professional organizations in various fields, including libraries, archives, museums, and historical institutions, could cooperate to sponsor such activities for their respective members.

Internships

Internships can provide another source of continuing education in the area of preservation. Information about formal internships can be found in professional journals for librarians and archivists. Internships might be available for credit through a school of library and information management or a program of archival studies in an academic institution.

An informal internship might be arranged in a library, an archive, or a museum that is willing to have its staff spend a limited period of time teaching a librarian or a small group of librarians about a specific aspect of preservation. For example, I spent a very profitable afternoon at the art museum of a major state university learning how their staff mats, frames, and stores artwork, as well as how the artwork is packed for shipment to exhibits.

Print and Audiovisual Resources

Publications and audiovisual resources can also provide a basis for continuing education in the field of preservation. The American Library Association, the Society of American Archivists, and the Association for State and Local History actively publish books and periodicals in this area. Publications relevant to preservation and conservation are also issued by other professional organizations, academic institutions, special libraries, museums, and governmental agencies. A highly selective list for further reading is appended to this chapter.

Audiovisual materials can also be used effectively in courses, meetings, and workshops as well as for in-house training of library staff members. Many of the audiovisual materials listed in mediagraphies are available through rental or loan from film rental libraries. Such materials as the excellent film *Slow Fires: On the Preservation of the Human Record* are invaluable in raising the consciousness of professionals, students, and laypeople. *Slow Fires,* which was sponsored by the Council on Library Resources, The National Endowment for the Humanities, and the Library of Congress, was originally shown on the Public Broadcasting System in 1987.

Internet Resources

Curators of special collections of children's literature can use electronic resources to assist them in continuing education, research, reading, involvement in professional organizations, and networking. Jane Hedberg's column, "Preservation News," which appears in *College and Research Libraries News,* is an excellent source of information about electronic resources as well as more-traditional resources in preservation. Curators exploring these resources will find valuable information and links to other relevant sites and databases.

Conservation DistList (Cons DistList), which was established in 1987, is an electronic discussion group available on the Internet to those professionals involved with the conservation of materials in libraries, archives, and museums. Subscribers can learn about preservation issues, funding opportunities, meetings, conferences, and educational opportunities. Walter Henry of the Stanford University Libraries is the list owner and moderator.

Conservation Online (CoOL) was also created by Walter Henry and is a collection of full-text databases concerning the preservation of materials in libraries, archives, and museums. CoOL includes the file list and E-mail directory for Cons DistList as well as documents from various organizations and individuals in the field of conservation. The Cons DistList can be accessed at http://palimpsest.stanford.edu. Subscription requests can be submitted to condist-request@lindy.stanford.edu. *The Abbey Newsletter,* a distinguished journal in the field of preservation, has a home page in CoOL.

Robert DeCandido, head of the shelf and binding preparation office at the New York Public Library, has created a Web site for the Preservation and Reformatting Section (PARS) of the Association for Library Collections & Technical Services for preservation information and PARS documents. It is available at http://www.well.com/user/bronxbob/pars/pars.html or the page can be accessed through the link at CoOL.

DeCandido also maintains a Web site for the Preservation Educators' Exchange (PRESED-X). It has been expanded to include not only syllabi of preservation courses but also training and educational opportunities and documents on topics that are of interest to those concerned about preservation. This Web site can be accessed at http://www.well.com/user/bronxbob/presed-x.html through Mosaic or Netscape. The best access to the graphics is through Netscape 1.1. Robert DeCandido can be contacted at bronxbob@well.com.

Other academic institutions are using the Internet in a variety of creative ways in the field of preservation. An online database of preservation documents associated with the FLIPPER listserv, "Florida Libraries Interested in Preservation Programs, Education and Resources," is available through electronic mail from the George A. Smathers Library Preservation Department at the University of Florida. Information can be obtained from ERIKESS@NERVM.NERDC.UFL.EDU on the Internet or ERIKESS@NERVM on Bitnet. The URL for the University of Florida is http://karamelik.eastlib.ufl.edu.

Grant funds from the National Center for Preservation Technology and Training have been used by the Dartmouth College Library to develop conservation training for the World Wide Web. A simple book-repair manual can be located at http://www.dartmouth.edu/~library/projects.html/.

Preservation and Conservation Studies (PCS) at the Graduate School of Library and Information Science at the University of Texas at Austin includes information about the program and hot links to other sites on its home page. The URL is http://volvo.gslis.utexas.edu/~PCS/pcshome.html.

Other library agencies have also found valuable ways to present helpful information on the Internet. The Western New York Library Resources Council (WNYLRC) has placed the 1994 edition of *Western New York Disaster Preparedness and Recovery Manual for Libraries and Archives* on the Internet at http://www.wnylrc.org/pub/disman.htm. Some of the information is relevant to institutions in other areas of the country.

Preservation Services of the Southeastern Library Network (SOLINET) includes information about workshops, a listing of publications available for sale, the full text of bibliographies and leaflets that are available free, and brief preservation articles. This home page is accessible through http://www.solinet.net/presvtn/preshome.htm.

Curators of special collections of children's literature who are responsible for the preservation of films, videos, and other formats with moving images will find the Association of Moving Image Archivists' online discussion list (AMIA-L) to be a valuable resource. To subscribe to AMIA-L, send an E-mail message to Listserv@lsv.uky.edu with the request: subscribe AMIA-L [your name]. The URL of AMIA is http://www.sc.library.unh.edu/amia/amia.htm.

Preservation resources in other countries are also available on the Internet. The Canadian Conservation Institute (CCI), a special operating agency of the Department of Canadian Heritage, has created a home page that includes information about conservation treatments, publications, scheduled events, and the CCI newsletter in full text. Access this source of valuable information at http://www.pch.gc.ca/cci-icc/.

A World Wide Web site and a discussion list are available for the European Commission on Preservation and Access at http://www.library.knaw.nl/epic/ecpatex/welcome.htm. The preservation journal *Restaurator* can be accessed through the Web site for the European Commission on Preservation and Access. Subscribe to the discussion list by sending the message: subscribe EPIC- LST [your name] to listserv@nic.surfnet.nl.

Commercial firms also provide preservation information on the Internet. Eastman Kodak includes information about the preservation of CDs and CD-ROM media on its home page (http://www.Kodak.com/daiHome/techInfo/permanence.html).

Electronic journals provide a convenient way for curators of special collections of children's literature to stay up-to-date on developments in preservation. The Association for Library Collections & Technical Services (ALCTS), a division of the American Library Association, publishes ALCTS Network News: AN2 several times a month. It provides news about ALCTS and relevant subjects such as programs and continuing education. The subscription address is listproc@ala.org.

Journals concerning preservation and indexes, such as *Library Literature,* that access preservation literature are available through online subscription services such as OCLC FirstSearch, Expanded Academic Index in Information Access Corporation (IAC), and Wilson OnLine. Document delivery is available through such electronic subscription services as Carl UnCover and EBSCODOC.

Disaster-Recovery Network

The Western Conservation Congress, organized in 1980, grew out of the Western States Materials Conservation Project. Chapters were established in the twenty states that were members of the Western Council of State Libraries, and a disaster resource person was trained for each state to consult with librarians who were preparing disaster plans, to present workshops, and to provide advice in coping with disasters. These librarians were not paid for their services by the Western Conservation Congress, but each person's institution could provide release time or travel expenses. The institution that needed the services might also reimburse the disaster resource person for services rendered.

CASE STUDY OF PRESERVATION NETWORKING

The importance of networking can best be illustrated by the following report. Acetate artwork held in the May Massee Collection was seriously deteriorating. In an attempt to solve this preservation problem, we contacted a number of specialists.

We first conferred with the director of a regional conservation center. Next, we consulted the archivist of a major motion picture studio because of the possible relationship between the acetate used in our deteriorating artwork and the cells that are used in animated films. The archivist referred us to a conservation laboratory in California.

The conservator at the laboratory asked for complete information about the environment of the collection as well as small samples of the acetate that we provided by overnight mail. After he performed tests in the laboratory, he phoned us the next day to give us information about the causes of deterioration. Factors included the nature of the acetate and chemical reactions caused by the polyvinyl chloride sleeves in which the artwork had been placed many years ago. The environment in the rooms where the artwork was stored also aggravated the deterioration. As a result, the conservator had discovered contact deterioration, dehydration, and accelerated aging due to the collection's environment and the use of polyvinyl chloride sleeves.

The conservator referred us to another conservator at a major art museum in California, who provided more background information and informed us of a relevant report that we were able to obtain through interlibrary loan. We were also referred to a conservator at the Nelson Gallery of Art and the Atkins Museum of Fine Arts in Kansas City who was writing an article concerning acetate artwork.

Other contact people in our rapidly expanding network of experts included the preservation officer at the Central Plains Regional Branch of the National Archives in Kansas City as well as members of the conservation staffs at the Library of Congress and the National Archives and Records Administration in Washington, D.C. Personnel at the latter institution had conducted preservation workshops sponsored by the Society of American Archivists and the American Association for State and Local History that I had attended. Those enrolled in the workshops had been encouraged to call the instructors if they needed advice about preservation problems.

The willingness to help and the concern expressed by everyone who was part of our network were impressive. The experts generously gave of their time and talent without compensation. The only expenses in addition to staff time were for phone calls and postage. However, armed with excellent advice, we finally came up against a major obstacle—a lack of financial resources to remedy the problem. Further consulting services, an on-site visit by a conservator, or actual conservation work would have required funding that was unavailable.

We contacted a number of agencies and corporations that might be possible sources of funding. Unfortunately, our project did not meet their guidelines. However, we were able to secure some funding from the Endowment Fund for the May Massee Collection and from the office of the president at Emporia State University. This funding allowed us to remove the destructive polyvinyl chloride sleeves from the more than 5,000 pieces of artwork, and interleave the pieces with archival-quality paper, a procedure recommended as a temporary measure. Sufficient funds were not available for appropriate matting of the artwork.

The lesson learned was that if those responsible for special collections of children's literature would consult with a conservator during the early stages of organization, measures could be taken to avoid the development of similar problems. The expenditure of funds for an on-site visit by a conservator would be less expensive than dealing with a serious preservation problem in the future. In addition, those responsible for a collection must follow the consultant's advice about the environment and the housing provided for a collection.

Referral Services

The Conservation Services Referral System is a free service available from the Foundation of the American Institute for Conservation of Historic and Artistic Works (FAIC). A list of professional conservators who are members of AIC will be provided. The list is organized by type of service, specialization, and geographic area to meet the needs of institutions and individuals.

Regional Conservation Associations, recognized by the American Institute for Conservation of Historic and Artistic Works, also provide referrals to professional conservators and provide information about conservation to interested institutions and individuals. Many of these associations also welcome members who are interested in conservation. A list of regional conservation associations is provided in appendix B at the end of this chapter.

Librarians who are seriously interested in the field of preservation can educate themselves through the methods presented in this chapter, so that they will be more knowledgeable curators of the resources for which they are responsible. They can preserve the treasures of children's literature to share with this and future generations.

Notes

1. National Conservation Advisory Council, *Conservation of Cultural Property in the United States: A Statement* (Washington, D.C.: National Conservation Advisory Council, 1976), 31.
2. Paul Conway, "Archival Preservation: Definitions for Improving Education and Training," *Restaurator* 10, no. 2 (1989): 47–50.
3. Karl E. Longstreth, "The Preservation of Library Materials in 1989: A Review of the Literature," *Library Resources & Technical Services* 34 (Oct. 1990): 461–2.
4. Mary Lynn Ritzenthaler, *Preserving Archives and Manuscripts* (Chicago: Society of American Archivists, 1984).
5. Mary Lynn Ritzenthaler, Gerald J. Munoff, and Margery S. Long,

Archives and Manuscripts: Administration of Photographic Collections (Chicago: Society of American Archivists, 1984); Gail E. Farr, *Archives and Manuscripts: Exhibits* (Chicago: Society of American Archivists, 1980).

6. Deanna B. Marcum, *Preservation Education Institute Final Report: August 2–4, 1990, from School of Library and Information Science, the Catholic University of America* (Washington, D.C.: Commission on Preservation and Access, 1990).

Further Reading

Bibliographies

Banks, Paul N. *A Selective Bibliography on the Conservation of Research Library Materials.* Chicago: Newberry Library, 1981.

Boomgaarden, Wesley L. "Preservation." In *Guide to Technical Services Resources,* edited by Peggy Johnson, 166–95. Chicago: American Library Assoc., 1994.

Cunha, George M., and Dorothy Grant Cunha. *Conservation of Library Materials: A Manual and Bibliography on the Care, Repair and Restoration of Library Materials.* Vol. 2. 2d ed. Metuchen, N.J.: Scarecrow, 1972.

———. *Library and Archives Conservation: 1980s and Beyond.* Vol. 2, *Bibliography.* Metuchen, N.J.: Scarecrow, 1983.

Drewes, Jeanne M. "A Widening Circle: Preservation Literature Review, 1992." *Library Resources & Technical Services* 37 (July 1993): 315–22.

Ericson, Timothy L., and Linda J. Ebben, comps. *Audiovisuals for Archivists.* Chicago: Society of American Archivists, 1985.

Fox, Lisa L., ed., Don K. Thompson and Joan Ten Hoor, comps. *A Core Collection in Preservation.* 2d ed. Chicago: American Library Assoc., Assoc. for Library Collections & Technical Services, 1993.

Harrison, Alice W., Edward A. Collister, and R. Ellen Willis. *The Conservation of Archival and Library Materials: A Resource Guide to Audiovisual Aids.* Metuchen, N.J.: Scarecrow, 1982.

Morrow, Carolyn Clark, and Steven B. Schoenly. *A Conservation Bibliography for Librarians, Archivists, and Administrators.* Troy, N.Y.: Whitson, 1979.

Murray, Toby, comp. *Bibliography on Disasters, Disaster Preparedness, and Disaster Recovery.* Tulsa, Okla.: Univ. of Tulsa, 1993.

Palmer, Joseph W. "Audiovisual Programs Related to Preservation: A Mediagraphy." *Collection Building* 13, no. 1 (1993):7–20.

Reese, Rosemary S., comp. *Care and Conservation of Collections.* Vol. 2, *A Bibliography on Historical Organization Practices.* Edited by Frederick L. Rath Jr. and Merrilyn Rogers O'Connell. Nashville, Tenn.: American Assoc. for State and Local History, 1977.

Society of American Archivists, Preservation Section, Education Committee. *Selected Readings in Preservation, 1993 and 1994.* Chicago: Society of American Archivists, 1996.

Swartzburg, Susan G. "Audiovisual Aids on the Preservation and Conservation of Library and Archival Materials." *Conservation Administration News* 49 (Apr. 1992): 8–13.

Books

Baker, John P., and Marguerite C. Soroka, eds. *Library Conservation: Preservation in Perspective.* Stroudsburg, Pa.: Dowden, Hutchinson & Ross, 1978.

Barton, John P., and Johanna C. Wellheiser, eds. *An Ounce of Prevention: A Handbook on Disaster Contingency Planning for Archives, Libraries and Record Centres.* Toronto: Toronto Area Archivists Group Education Foundation, 1985.

Boyle, Deidre. *Video Preservation: Securing the Future of the Past.* New York: Media Alliance, 1993.

Child, Margaret S., comp. *Directory of Information Sources on Scientific Research Related to the Preservation of Sound Recordings, Still and Moving Images and Magnetic Tape.* Washington, D.C.: Commission on Preservation and Access, 1993.

Clapp, Anne F. *Curatorial Care of Works of Art on Paper: Basic Procedures for Paper Preservation.* 4th rev. ed. New York: Nick Lyons Books, 1987.

Coleman, Christopher D. G. *Preservation Education Directory.* 7th ed. Chicago: American Library Assoc., Assoc. for Library Collections & Technical Services, Preservation of Library Materials Section, Education Committee, 1995.

Darling, Pamela W., and Duane Webster. *Preservation Planning Program: An Assisted Self-Study Manual for Libraries.* Revised by Jan Merrill-Oldham and Jutta Reed-Scott. Washington, D.C.: Assoc. of Research Libraries, Office of Management Services, 1993.

Edwards, Stephen R., Bruce M. Bell, and Mary Elizabeth King, comps. *Pest Control in Museums: A Status Report (1980).* Lawrence, Kans.: Assoc. of Systematics Collections, 1981.

Elkington, Nancy E., ed. *Digital Imaging Technology for Preservation: Proceedings from an RLG Symposium Held March 17 and 18, 1994, Cornell University, Ithaca, New York.* Mountain View, Calif.: Research Libraries Group, 1994.

————. *RLG Archives Microfilming Manual.* Mountain View, Calif.: Research Libraries Group, 1994.

Ellis, Margaret Holben. *The Care of Prints and Drawings.* Walnut Creek, Calif.: AltaMira Pr., 1995.

Fortson, Judith. *Disaster Planning and Recovery: A How-to-Do-It Manual for Librarians and Archivists.* New York: Neal-Schuman, 1992.

Fox, Lisa, ed. *Preservation Microfilming: A Guide for Librarians and Archivists.* 2d ed. Chicago: American Library Assoc., 1996.

Henderson, Kathryn Luther, and William T. Henderson, eds. *Conserving and Preserving Materials in Nonbook Formats.* Allerton Park Institute, no. 30. Urbana-Champaign: Univ. of Ill., Graduate School of Library and Information Science, 1991.

Higginbotham, Barbara Buckner, ed. *Advances in Preservation and Access.* Vol. 2. Medford, N.J.: Learned Information, 1995.

Higginbotham, Barbara Buckner, and Mary E. Jackson, eds. *Advances in Preservation and Access.* Vol. 1. Westport, Conn.: Meckler, 1992.

Horton, Carolyn. *Cleaning and Preserving Bindings and Related Materials.* 2d ed. revised. LTP Publications #16. Chicago: American Library Assoc., 1978.

Jones, Norvell M. M., and Mary Lynn Ritzenthaler. "Implementing an Archival Preservation Program." In *Managing Archives and Archival Institutions,* 185–206. Chicago: Univ. of Chicago Pr., 1988.

Kahn, Miriam. *Disaster Response and Planning for Libraries.* Chicago: American Library Assoc., 1998.

———. *First Steps for Handling and Drying Water-Damaged Materials.* Columbus, Ohio: MBK Consulting, 1994.

Lull, William P., and Paul N. Banks. *Conservation Environment Guidelines for Libraries and Archives.* Ottawa: Canadian Council of Archives, 1995.

Morris, John. *The Library Disaster Preparedness Handbook.* Chicago: American Library Assoc., 1986.

Morrow, Carolyn Clark. "Preservation Comes of Age." In *Library and Book Trade Almanac,* 71–6. 1989–90. 34th ed. New York: R. R. Bowker, 1989.

Morrow, Carolyn Clark, with Gay Walker. *The Preservation Challenge: A Guide to Conserving Library Materials.* White Plains, N.Y.: Knowledge Industry, 1983.

Morrow, Carolyn Clark, Carole Dyal, and Todd C. Matus. *Conservation Treatment Procedures: A Manual of Step-by-Step Procedures for the Maintenance and Repair of Library Materials.* 2d ed. Littleton, Colo.: Libraries Unlimited, 1986.

New York University Libraries, Preservation Committee. *Disaster Plan Workbook.* New York: NYU Libraries, 1984.

Oakley, Robert L. *Copyright and Preservation: A Serious Problem in Need of a Thoughtful Solution.* Washington, D.C.: Commission on Preservation and Access, 1990.

Ogden, Sherelyn, ed. *Preservation of Library and Archival Materials: A Manual.* 2d ed. Washington, D.C.: American Assoc. of Museums, Technical Information Service, 1994.

Paris, Jan. *Choosing and Working with a Conservator.* Atlanta, Ga.: SOLINET Preservation Program, Southeastern Library Network, 1990.

Price, Lois Olcott. *Mold: Managing a Mold Invasion: Guidelines for Disaster Response.* Technical Series, no. 1. Philadelphia: Conservation Center for Art and Historic Artifacts, 1996.

A Primer on Disaster Preparedness, Management, and Response Paper-Bases Materials: Selected Reprints. Washington, D.C.: Smithsonian Institution, 1993. Also available through Conservation Online (CoOL).

SAA Education Directory (Annual). Chicago: Society of American Archivists.

Scham, A. M. *Managing Special Collections.* New York: Neal-Schuman, 1987.

Swartzburg, Susan G. "Preservation of Sound Recordings." In *Encyclopedia of Recorded Sound in the United States.* Edited by Guy A. Marco, 542–6. New York: Garland, 1993.

———. *Preserving Library Materials: A Manual.* 2d ed. Metuchen, N.J.: Scarecrow, 1995.

Swartzburg, Susan G., ed. *Conservation in the Library: A Handbook of Use and Care of Traditional and Nontraditional Materials.* Westport, Conn.: Greenwood, 1983.

Trinkaus-Randall, Gregor. *Protecting Your Collections: A Manual of Archival Security.* Chicago: Society of American Archivists, 1995.

Trinkley, Michael. *Can You Stand the Heat? A Fire Safety Primer for Libraries, Archives and Museums.* Atlanta, Ga.: Southeastern Library Network, 1993.

Waters, Peter. *Procedures for Salvage of Water-Damaged Library Materials.* 2d ed. Washington, D.C.: Library of Congress, 1979.

Wilhelm, Henry Gilmer, with Carol Brower. *The Permanence and Care of Color Photographs: Traditional and Digital Color Prints, Color Negatives, Slides and Motion Pictures.* Grinnell, Iowa: Preservation, 1993.

Monographs

ARL Preservation Statistics. Washington, D.C.: Assoc. of Research Libraries, 1987–1988.

Association of Research Libraries, Office of Management Services. *Automating Preservation Management in ARL Libraries.* SPEC Kit #198. Washington, D.C.: Assoc. of Research Libraries, Dec. 1993.

———. *Basic Preservation Procedures.* SPEC Kit #70. Washington, D.C.: Assoc. of Research Libraries, Jan. 1981.

———. *Brittle Books Programs.* SPEC Kit #152. Washington, D.C.: Assoc. of Research Libraries, Mar. 1989.

———. *The Changing Role of Book Repair.* SPEC Kit #190. Washington, D.C.: Assoc. of Research Libraries, Apr. 1993.

————. *Collection Security.* SPEC Kit #100. Washington, D.C.: Assoc. of Research Libraries, Jan. 1984.

————. *Digitizing Technologies for Preservation.* SPEC Kit #214. Washington, D.C.: Assoc. of Research Libraries, Mar. 1996.

————. *Organizing for Preservation.* SPEC Kit #116. Washington, D.C.: Assoc. of Research Libraries, July/Aug. 1985.

————. *Planning for Preservation.* SPEC Kit #66. Washington, D.C.: Assoc. of Research Libraries, July/Aug. 1980.

————. *Preparing for Emergencies and Disasters.* SPEC Kit #69. Washington, D.C.: Assoc. of Research Libraries, Nov./Dec. 1980.

————. *Preservation Education in ARL Libraries.* SPEC Kit #113. Washington, D.C.: Assoc. of Research Libraries, Apr. 1985.

————. *Preservation Guidelines in ARL Libraries.* SPEC Kit #137. Washington, D.C.: Assoc. of Research Libraries, Sept. 1987.

————. *Preservation of Library Materials.* SPEC Kit #35. Washington, D.C.: Assoc. of Research Libraries, Aug. 1977.

————. *Preservation Organization and Staffing.* SPEC Kit #160. Washington, D.C.: Assoc. of Research Libraries, Jan. 1990.

Banks, Jennifer. *Options for Replacing and Reformatting Deteriorated Materials.* Washington, D.C.: Assoc. of Research Libraries, 1993.

Boomgaarden, Wesley. *Staff Training and User Awareness in Preservation Management.* Washington, D.C.: Assoc. of Research Libraries, 1993.

Brooks, Constance. *Disaster Preparedness.* Washington, D.C.: Assoc. of Research Libraries, 1993.

Byrne, Sherry. *Collection Maintenance and Improvement.* Washington, D.C.: Assoc. of Research Libraries, 1993.

Cloonan, Michelle. *Organizing Preservation Activities.* Washington, D.C.: Assoc. of Research Libraries, 1993.

DeCandido, Robert. *Collections Conservation.* Washington, D.C.: Assoc. of Research Libraries, 1993.

George, Susan C. *Emergency Planning and Management in College Libraries.* ACRL CLIP Note #17. Chicago: American Library Assoc., Assoc. of College and Research Libraries, College Libraries Section, College Library Information Packet Committee, 1994.

LaFontaine, Raymond H. *Environmental Norms for Canadian Muse-*

ums, *Art Galleries and Archives.* Technical Bulletin 5. Rev. and corrected ed. Ottawa: Canadian Conservation Institute, 1981.

————. *Recommended Environmental Monitors for Museums, Galleries and Archives.* Technical Bulletin 3. Rev. ed. Ottawa: Canadian Conservation Institute, 1980.

LaFontaine, Raymond H., and Patricia A. Wood. *Fluorescent Lamps. Technical Bulletin 7.* Rev. ed. Ottawa: Canadian Conservation Institute, 1982.

Library of Congress. Preservation Office. Preservation Leaflets. Washington, D.C.: Library of Congress, 1975– .

 #1 *Selected References in the Literature of Conservation,* 1975.

 #2 *Environmental Protection of Books and Related Materials,* 1979.

 #3 *Preserving Leather Bookbindings,* 1975.

 #4 *Marking Paper Manuscripts,* 1983.

 #5 *Preserving Newspapers and Newspaper-Type Materials,* 1977.

Macleod, Kenneth J. *Museum Lighting.* Technical Bulletin 2. Ottawa: Canadian Conservation Institute, 1978.

————. *Relative Humidity: Its Importance, Measurement, and Control in Museums.* Technical Bulletin 1. Ottawa: Canadian Conservation Institute, 1978.

Merrill-Oldham, Jan. *Managing a Library Binding Program.* Washington, D.C.: Assoc. of Research Libraries, 1993.

Strang, Thomas J. K. *Controlling Museum Fungal Problems.* Technical Bulletin 12. Ottawa: Canadian Conservation Institute, 1991.

Strang, Thomas J. K., and John E. Dawson. *Controlling Vertebrate Pests in Museums.* Technical Bulletin 13. Ottawa: Canadian Conservation Institute, 1991.

————. *Solving Museum Insect Problems: Chemical Control.* Technical Bulletin 15. Ottawa: Canadian Conservation Institute, 1992.

Articles

The American Archivist (Special Preservation Issue) 53 (spring 1990):184–369.

Banks, Paul N. "Environmental Standards for Storage of Books and Manuscripts." *Library Journal* 99 (1 Feb. 1974): 339–43.

Berger, Pearl. "Minor Repairs in a Small Research Library." *Library Journal* 104 (15 June 1979): 1311–17.

Bohem, Hilda. "Regional Conservation Services: What Can We Do for Ourselves?" *Library Journal* 104 (July 1979): 1428–31.

The Bookmark (Conservation/Preservation Issue) 45 (spring 1987): 138–93.

"Colloquium on Preservation." *Oklahoma Librarian* 30 (Oct. 1980): 11–41.

Darling, Pamela W. "A Local Preservation Program: Where to Start?" *Library Journal* 101 (15 Nov. 1976): 2343–7.

Jermann, Peter. "Implications of Electronic Formats for Preservation Administrators." *Commission on Preservation and Access Newsletter* (Nov.–Dec. 1993): 2-page insert.

Kahn, Miriam. "Mastering Disaster: Emergency Planning for Libraries." *Library Journal* 118 (Dec. 1993): 73–5.

McCrady, Ellen. "Mold as a Threat to Human Health." *The Abbey Newsletter* 18 (1994): 65–6.

Pence, Cheryl. "Audiovisual Resources on Preservation Topics." *The American Archivist* 53 (spring 1990): 350–4.

Raphael, Toby J. "The Care of Leather and Skin Products: A Curator's Guide." *Leather Conservation News* 9 (1993): 1–15.

Reich, Vicky, Connie Brooks, Willy Cromwell, and Scott Wicks. "Electronic Discussion Lists and Journals: A Guide for Technical Services Staff." *Library Resources & Technical Services* 39 (July 1995): 303–19.

APPENDIX A

Preservation Periodicals

*The Abbey Newsletter: Bookbinding
   and Conservation*
Abbey Publications, Inc.
7105 Geneva Dr.
Austin, TX 78723-1510

AIC News
American Institute for
   Conservation of Historic
   and Artistic Works
1717 K St. NW, Ste. 301
Washington, DC 20006-1501

ALCTS Newsletter
Assoc. for Library Collections
   & Technical Services
American Library Assoc.
50 E. Huron St.
Chicago, IL 60611-2795

American Archivist
Society of American Archivists
600 S. Federal St., Ste. 504
Chicago, IL 60605-1898

Archival Outlook
Society of American Archivists
600 S. Federal St., Ste. 504
Chicago, IL 60605-1898

Art Documentation
Art Libraries Society of N. Am.
4101 Lake Boone Tr., Ste. 201
Raleigh, NC 27607-7506

*College and Research Libraries
   News*
Assoc. of College and Research
   Libraries
American Library Assoc.
50 E. Huron St.
Chicago, IL 60611- 2795

*Commission on Preservation
   and Access Newsletter*
Commission on Preservation
   and Access
Council on Library and
   Information Resources
1400 16th St. NW, Ste. 740
Washington, DC 20036-2217

*Conservation Administration News:
   Library and Archival
   Preservation (CAN)*
Univ. of Texas at Austin
Graduate School of Library
   and Information Science,
   Preservation and Conservation
   Studies
EDB 564
Austin, TX 78712-1276

History News
American Assoc. for State
   and Local History
530 Church St., Ste. 600
Nashville, TN 37219-2325

*Infinity: The Newsletter of the SAA
   Preservation Section*
Preservation Section
Society of American Archivists
600 S. Federal St., Ste. 504
Chicago, IL 60605-1898

Library & Archival Security
Haworth Press, Inc.
10 Alice St.
Binghamton, NY 13904

Library Resources & Technical
  Services
Assoc. for Library Collections
  & Technical Services
American Library Assoc.
50 E. Huron St.
Chicago, IL 60611-2795

Microform and Imaging Review
K. G. Saur, Verlag KG
Ortlerstr 8
81373 Munich, Germany
Distributed in U.S. by R. R. Bowker
121 Chanlon Rd.
New Providence, NJ 07974

The New Library Scene
Library Binding Institute
7401 Metro Blvd., Ste. 325
Edina, MN 55439-3031

Restaurator: International Journal
  for the Preservation
  of Library and Archival Material
Munksgaard Intl. Publishers Ltd.
35 Nørre Søgade
P. O. Box 2148
DK-1016 Copenhagen K, Denmark

Technology and Conservation
  of Art, Architecture and
  Antiquities
Technology Organization, Inc.
76 Highland Ave.
Somerville, MA 02143

APPENDIX B

Organizations and Institutions
with Preservation Concerns

**American Assoc. for State and
Local History (AASLH)**
530 Church St., Ste. 600
Nashville, TN 37219-2325
(615) 255-2971
Fax: (615) 255-2979
E-mail: aaslh@nashville.net
http://www.nashville.net/~aaslh

**American Assoc. of Museums
(AAM)**
1575 I St. NW, Ste. 400
Washington, DC 20005
(202) 289-1818
Fax: (202) 289-6578
http://www.americanmuse.org/aam

**American Institute for
Conservation of Historic
and Artistic Works (AIC)**
1717 K St. NW, Ste. 301
Washington, DC 20006-1501
(202) 452-9545
Fax: (202) 452-9328
E-mail: infoaic@aol.com

**Assoc. for Library Collections
& Technical Services**
American Library Assoc. (ALA)
50 E. Huron St.
Chicago, IL 60611-2795
(800) 545-2433 Ext. 5038
Fax: (312) 280-3257
E-mail: alcts@ala.org
http://www.ala.org/alcts.html

**Assoc. of Research Libraries
(ARL)**
21 Dupont Cir. NW, Ste. 800
Washington, DC 20036

(202) 296-2296
Fax: (202) 872-0884
E-mail: duane@cni.org
http://arl.cni.org

**Balboa Art Conservation Ctr.
(BACC)**
P. O. Box 3755
San Diego, CA 92163-1755
(619) 236-9702
Fax: (619) 236-0141

**Bay Area Art Conservation
Group**
c/o Margaret Geiss-Mooney
1124 Clelia Ct.
Petaluma, CA 94954-5617
(707) 763-8694

**Chicago Area Conservation
Group**
c/o Craig Deller, Pres.
260 Keslinger Rd.
Geneva, IL 60134-3908
(630) 232-1708
Fax: (630) 232-0937
E-mail: craig1708@aol.com

**Commission on Preservation
and Access (CPA)**
Council of Library and Information
Resources
1400 16th St. NW, Ste. 740
Washington, DC 20036-2217
(202) 939-3400
Fax: (202) 939-3407
E-mail: mksitts@cpa.org
http://www.cpa.stanford.edu/
cpa.html

**Conservation Associates
of the Pacific Northwest
(CAP Northwest)**
P. O. Box 2756
Olympia, WA 98507-2756
(360) 754-2093
Fax: (360) 754-2093
E-mail: dr_cpr_llc@juno.com

**Conservation Ctr. for Art &
Historic Artifacts (CCAHA)**
264 S. 23rd St.
Philadelphia, PA 19103-5530
(215) 545-0613
Fax: (215) 735-9313
E-mail: ccaha@shrsys.hslc.org
http://www.ccaha.org

Gerald R. Ford Conservation Ctr.
1326 S. 32nd St.
Omaha, NE 68105
(402) 595-1180
Fax: (402) 595-1178
E-mail: grfcc@radiks.net

Guild of Book Workers (GBW)
521 Fifth Ave.
New York, NY 10175
(212) 292-4444

Image Permanence Institute (IPI)
Rochester Institute of Technology
70 Lomb Memorial Dr.
Rochester, NY 14623-5604
(716) 475-5199
Fax: (716) 475-7230
E-mail: jmrpph@rit.edu

**Intermuseum Conservation
Assoc. (ICA)**
Allen Art Bldg.
83 N. Main St.
Oberlin, OH 44074-1192
(216) 775-7331
Fax: (216) 774-3431

Library of Congress (LC) LM-G21
101 Independence Ave., SE
Preservation Directorate
Washington, DC 20540-4500
(202) 707-5213
Fax: (202) 707-3434
E-mail: nppo@loc.gov
http://www.loc.gov

**Louisiana Art Conservation
Alliance**
P. O. Box 71473
New Orleans, LA 70172-1473

**Midwest Regional Conservation
Guild (MRCG)**
c/o Nicola J. Longford
Missouri Historical Society
P. O. Box 11940
St. Louis, MO 63112-0040
(314) 746-4543
Fax: (314) 746-4548

**National Archives and Records
Admin. (NARA)**
Document Conservation Branch
8601 Adelphi Rd.
College Park, MD 20740-6001
(301) 713-6700
Fax: (301) 713-7466
E-mail: preserve@nara.gov
http://www.nara.gov

**National Institute for the
Conservation of Cultural
Property (NIC)**
3299 K St. NW, Ste. 602
Washington, DC 20007-4439
(202) 625-1495
Fax: (202) 625-1485
E-mail: info@nic.org
http://www.nic.org

**New England Conservation Assoc.
 (NECA)**
c/o Kathryn Myatt Carey
24 Emery St.
Medford, MA 02155
(617) 396-9495

New York Conservation Assoc.
c/o Jon Scott, Treas.
P. O. Box 20098 LT
New York, NY 10011
E-mail: jscott@panix.com

**New York State Office of Parks,
 Recreation and Historic
 Preservation**
Bureau of Historic Sites
Peebles Island
P. O. Box 219
Waterford, NY 12188-0219
(518) 237-8643
Fax: (518) 235-4248

**Northeast Document
 Conservation Ctr. (NEDCC)**
100 Brickstone Sq.
Andover, MA 01810-1494
(508) 470-1010
Fax: (508) 475-6021
E-mail: nedcc@nedcc.org
http://www.nedcc.org

**Rocky Mountain Conservation
 Ctr. (RMCC)**
2420 S. University Blvd.
Denver, CO 80208
(303) 733-2712

7

Using Children's Literature Special Collections

Margaret Maloney

To have many books, and never to use them, is like a child that will have a candle burning by him all the while he is sleeping.

—Henry Peacham, *The Compleat Gentleman,* 1622

The primary mandate for the staff of most active special collections is to identify, acquire, make accessible, and preserve the resources appropriate to support the interest and work of their perceived clientele.

Special collections of children's literature may be historical or contemporary or a mix of both. They may be channeled by specific focus of subject or of genre or even of format. Further limitations may be those of nationality or language represented. They may be chartered to serve a specific clientele or patron base: local tax-payers, a university community, or a political body or government constituency. Their institutions may be public, academic, educational, or cultural/historic (that is, gallery, museum, etc.). Users may be restricted geographically and permitted a range from limited to open access. Collections may include any combination of books, periodicals, ephemera, artwork, photographs, manuscripts, letters, archives, related objects or toys, "high tech" audiovisual records, and resource/reference material. They will attract interest as broad as the range of their subject matter and as diverse as the possibilities of approach they can offer. Queries may arise in person, by correspondence, by telephone, or by fax and other electronic media.

Users may include a broad and varied range of individual scholars, tourists, bibliophiles, people in business or the media and the arts, authors, editors, artists, publishers, performers, private collectors, dealers, advertisers, designers, and filmmakers. They may come from museums; galleries; libraries; and other educational, historical, and cultural agencies. Some special collections can accommodate groups: elementary, secondary, college, university, postgraduate, and special interest groups.

Special collections may serve a repository function. The increasing awareness of conservation, security, and space factors is inspiring authors, artists, and private collectors to look to responsible institutions as custodians of their archives for future research. A long-established and successful special collection is inevitably drawn into a consulting role. Staff from other organizations inquire about the implications of accepting large gifts, perhaps with conditions. Have they considered the cost not only in terms of staff, time, and space but also in the practical matters of access and a philosophical commitment to the future? They also ask advice about cataloging procedures, classification schemes, etc., and for support in grant applications. Libraries that have enjoyed long and constructive relationships with a Friends group are often asked to share their experience. If policy and administration are supportive and staffing is adequate, lectures and programs can be taken out into the community.

Special collections attract collectors in their specialized fields. Working with them is almost always mutually beneficial. True scholars and collectors tend to be generous with their discoveries and information exchanges. As more and more private collectors struggle with the cost and impact of insurance for fire, theft, and vandalism, they may decide to give part or all of their collections to the institutions that helped them build their collections. Collectors or colleagues setting up new collections are always grateful to those with experience at established institutions who will share not only subject information but cataloging methods, conservation techniques, dealer contacts, etc.

The media usually offer the opportunity for a symbiotic exchange. Those involved with film, television, and radio as well as newspapers and magazines look for unusual visually attractive features. Children's literature collections offer these in abundance in exchange for good public relations, gaining broad and free publicity at a populist level for their institutions. Libraries can provide textual and graphic material, notes on exciting new acquisitions, biographical information, seasonal nostalgia, etc. Occasionally they are sought out as actual sites for movie scenes, television, or still shots for programming or advertising. (With such major undertakings, be sure to have institutional approval and a precise contract including any payments, damage clauses, etc.)

Reading Room Facilities

Ideally, special collections reading rooms should be spacious, appropriately lit, secure, attractively appointed, adequately staffed, and equally inviting to the serious scholar and the casual tourist. Practically, many special collections reading rooms must inevitably compromise: cutting costs, stretching staff, cramping space, and recycling furniture. In other words, they must "make do" while cherishing the dream of what *could* be and indeed what *should* be. Never lose sight of that vision or dissipate the energy to achieve it.

There must be adequate room for both clientele and staff to work, affording the latter clear sight lines to oversee but not overwhelm the clientele. There should be good and correct task lighting that is easy to maintain. Furnishings should be comfortable and appropriate. Collections of more commonly available materials to be browsed can provide more casual seating, while research libraries must have chairs and work surfaces that also ensure the protection of the material. Scholars may have to put in eight-hour days for several weeks or months. Study carrels may accommodate long-term researchers but must be large enough for the materials, be properly lit, and be designed and positioned for surveillance. Maps, artwork, or folio volumes require format-oriented space and possibly support devices.

Rare book collections may provide long, thin fabric-wrapped weights—"snakes" or rolled futons—to hold open books. This minimizes handling and frees the reader to record. A ready supply of acid-free paper slips provides bookmarks for the readers' purposes and discourages other expediencies. Along with a supply of sharp pencils and call slips, any specific restrictions may be applied: clean hands or cloth gloves; no food or drink; no pens, ink, or tracing paper. Many libraries insist that patrons leave at the door (in lockers, racks, etc.) not only their outdoor clothing but also briefcases and handbags—a policy that necessitates a security-check system. If personal belongings *are* allowed in the reading room, they should remain segregated from library materials with which the patron is working. Patron registration—requiring name, address, phone, interest, and affiliation—can enhance security for the library and provide an acceptable link for the user to future discoveries. More-detailed call slips may also fill this function.

Use of Materials—Patron Perspective

The patron's primary concern is access. For casual visitors this means access to materials of interest and entertainment value. For serious researchers it means access to materials relevant to their area of work or study.

Access implies as easy identification and swift retrieval as possible. In a closed-stack library a short, clear reference interview with the inexperienced and perhaps unclear and unfocused researcher is paramount. Otherwise, both staff and patron waste time and energy. The better the users can define their queries or areas of interest and intent, the more effectively knowledgeable staff can respond.

Of additional value to the scholar is the opportunity to consider all useful items, even those among uncataloged backlog materials (which virtually every library has), new acquisitions, and on-order materials. The patron may be dependent on the accuracy of the cataloging data provided by the institution not only on-site but through electronic data, telephone, and correspondence. Errors, however inadvertently supplied, from a reputable source, particularly those in print or online, proliferate with time and repetition—a virtual Pandora's box.

Whether demanding or docile, patrons are usually grateful for staff assistance and often generous in sharing their own bibliographic insights and knowledge to add to the library's intellectual storehouse. Today's satisfied patron is often tomorrow's grateful benefactor—of contracts, ideas, and support, as well as financial or marginal gifts.

Physical Access

Access is of paramount importance. If a library holds some of the greatest treasures of the world but its appropriate clientele can neither determine these holdings nor physically use them, then the library becomes a moribund repository rather than a vital resource. The conjunction of important materials and effective yet responsible access is a prime incentive in generating creative scholarship.

It is essential that potential users have an immediate physical sense of the special collection they approach. Whether the stacks are open or closed or indeed primarily off-site, there should be, at least, evidence of the materials. Therefore, some books should be visible. They could be reference works, relevant periodicals or journals, facsimiles and reprints, or most effectively, an exhibition area for original materials either in display cases or on protected shelving. This visibility encourages all levels of clientele: the scholar who may see a new connection or approach, the casual visitor whose interest may focus and become engaged, and the donor who needs to be reassured that in this institution gifts are valued, used, conserved, and, as appropriate, publicly celebrated.

Closed Stacks

Compared with open stacks, closed stacks provide better security, regrettably a rising concern in all libraries. They give staff a greater measure of control and of order. Also greater freedom in physical arrangement is possible if the patrons do not retrieve materials themselves. Historical collections of old and fragile items are better protected from being handled casually or carelessly. Rare, unique, and ephemeral materials can be provided at the librarian's discretion.

All who work in special collections face the casual client who, when assistance is proffered, replies "No, thank you, I'd just like to browse." Even more problematic is the eminent scholar or visiting dignitary who asks that you "just open the stacks and let me browse." The answer must be clear and diplomatic but politely firm. If exceptions are made, how do you then explain rules, let alone enforce them with your next client who may have witnessed or been told about the joys of browsing?

Open Stacks

Open stacks could only work in a small, carefully and fully monitored room. It is difficult to supervise public retrieval and, despite posted admonitions, prevent reshelving. Will the inexperienced client reach for a physically fragile work and simply pull off the spine? Will a misguided "helper" misshelve a book that then becomes essentially lost to staff and public until a time-consuming search restores it? Besides damage and loss, open stacks increase the risk of vandalism and theft. Together these outweigh the specious arguments of lower costs and less staff and aesthetic or tactile benefits for patrons. A major consideration in determining the type of access offered to users must be the conditions that are covered by the institution's insurance policy.

Interlibrary Loans

Most special collections, certainly those holding unique, original, or rare and fragile materials, do *not* provide interlibrary loan services. The risk of damage or loss is too high. Insurance provisions must be examined and weighed in any consideration. Also, if an institution has a widely accessible catalog, the clientele assume that the holdings listed therein should be available for study on the premises.

Scholars generally accept the fact that they, rather than the works they wish to consult, must travel. Online networks such as ESTC (Eighteenth-Century Short Title Catalogue) pinpoint the only or most-convenient location. Many funding organizations facilitate such research trips.

Exhibition Loans

If libraries do not loan materials for individual use, they may selectively agree to contribute items to major exhibitions under the auspices of other institutions for a limited period of time. These may be culled from a collection of duplicates or, if the value of the lending library's involvement is significant in terms of contribution to a landmark catalog or to filling a scholarly gap, etc., they *may* loan prime pieces from their main collection. However, such items should not be gone too long (approximately two months maximum), and every assurance should be provided in writing with regard to insurance, security, lighting, and methods of display, packing, and conservation. For large and/or important loans, a senior staff member of the lending institution should monitor the procedure and attend the opening. It is wise also to note and ensure the accuracy of the publicity and acknowledgments. Any costs incurred are of course the responsibility of the borrower.

Loans that must cross borders—even undefended ones—can be problematic. Whenever possible, materials are best hand-carried by an interested party, preferably the lender. Customs brokers dine out on horror tales of warehouses, loading docks, and reversed or revised destinations! An experienced, reputable, and specialized broker should be used. All circumstances should be clarified and all the correct paperwork prepared for the reassurance of both the lender and borrower. Customs has the right to seize and impound! Be clear and truthful.

Photocopying

Photocopying must be a privilege, not a right. Many institutions do not provide *any* reproduction services. Some have such backlogs or delays or prohibitive costs as to be discouraging.

Photocopying of primary materials should never be done directly by the clientele. Trained library staff or their appropriate designates should undertake any reproduction. The client's purpose and use should be clearly determined.

Rare or fragile materials, particularly unique items, must be considered individually by a qualified professional. Manuscript materials or original artwork should *never* be photocopied. Requests for other forms of reproduction for publication or research should be directed for decision by the librarian in charge.

Not only can photocopying cause damage, it also may involve any applicable laws of copyright. The institution must protect not only the owner of any copyright—author or artist—but also its own integrity and reputation. The librarian (and by extension the library) who reproduces material that is under copyright is the one who infringes upon the law, *not* the client who requests it. With current tightening of this legislation, prosecution is more probable. Beware the client who may ask for a photocopy of a good, clear line drawing and is vague about its purpose. Fair quality reproductions can be achieved from such a photocopy, bypassing any fees or permissions for commercial use. Insist upon written documentation—clarifying purpose, contact person, company or institution, address, etc.

Reprints and Facsimiles

Reprints and facsimiles of works that already are or should be in a special collection are valuable resources for both staff and the public. While they may not satisfy the aesthetic sense of the true bibliophile or the pursuer of physical evidence, a reprint of the text is better than nothing at all, much cheaper and less fragile than the original, and may include a valuable critical commentary by an expert in the field. If a library deals with large groups of students, then such reprints, possibly several copies, become useful aids.

Special collections may also become directly involved with producing commercial facsimile projects. These also help to fund and advertise the library. The growing collection of facsimiles provides attractive, low-risk browsing and loan display materials. It is particularly inviting for young school children who may easily and safely examine works, the originals of which would be too frail or costly for unwarranted perusal.

Among the most successful series of reprints have been Milestones in Children's Literature (Oxford University Press), Garland Reprints, and Johnson Reprints and the two groups of facsimiles from the Osborne Collection published by Holp Shuppan in Tokyo (with one group reissued by the Bodley Head). Popular pictorial anthologies, although poorly documented and rarely indexed, serve a visual need.

Some libraries or their associated Friends groups sponsor and fund the publication of facsimiles from the special collections. These generate publicity and revenue, and when carefully chosen, foster scholarship. However, their production is time-consuming, especially for already-pressed staff. Their worth is greatly enhanced if a preface or end piece is added, establishing the work's importance and historical context. This reprint may then be offered as a gift or sold through membership to a support group. (Since 1966 the Friends of Osborne has annually sponsored the publication of a collection-related book for its membership.)

Exhibition Catalogs

Exhibition catalogs on specific themes or for special events are usually costly labors of love completed by knowledgeable staff, guest curators, or external experts whose insights provide invaluable information for students and scholars alike. Published lectures, particularly those with bibliographies, can shed new light on aspects of a collection. These types of publications, particularly if graphically enhanced, can become compelling tools for public relations, fund-raising, and political awareness.

Reproduction Rights

As commercial demands upon libraries escalate, the need for a clear and consistent policy on reproduction rights becomes essential. It must be a balanced choice. Few libraries charge scholars for research work or publication beyond the actual cost of reproduction (slide, photograph, etc.) and a modest service fee for handling and postage. However, publication for profit should incur a cost for the clients and a financial return to the institution. Publishers or their researchers are constant users of special collections of children's materials. They seek out-of-copyright text and graphics for reprints, anthologies, period pieces, etc. Institutions such as public or university libraries that have circumscribed clientele—their taxpayers or their student and faculty bodies—cannot justify substantial commitment of their staff and operational time to supporting a specific commercial venture without jeopardizing their primary mission.

Over the past decade a resurgence of nostalgia for Victoriana has fueled requests for graphics suitable for greeting card designs, specifically Christmas images, and for illustrations to be reproduced as gift wrap, textile patterns, or wallpaper friezes. Individuals have sought appropriate choices for calendars, bookplates, bookmarks, corporate logos, etc. Theater, music, and dance companies have used materials for scripts, costumes, sets, advertising, and programs. From marginal or nonprofit groups of cultural content, the institution can hope for little more than good public relations and published credit acknowledgment.

Methods of Security

To mark, deface, or electronically tag a fragile, original work is at best a contradiction and at worst a travesty. Most of the regular research library protective routines—checking or monitoring bags and outdoor clothing and prohibiting eating or drinking (no mud, jam, or chocolate), ink, ballpoint, tracing paper, scissors, etc.—have been mentioned elsewhere as have such positive measures as patron registration, reference letters, request slips, etc. In addition to these more-obvious, common-sense precautions, serious rare book collections require the protection of a highly technical and professional security system. Adequate staff supervision is essential. Also required are alarm-fitted exterior emergency doors during open hours and a motion detector that signals a central security unit with a quick, effective, and guaranteed response time that is in effect during hours when the collection is closed.

Adequate fire protection should be ensured using sophisticated smoke detectors with whatever combination of gas (halon, etc.) or sprinkler system is chosen that is environmentally and politically correct. The response required should be tied to the degree of threat.

It is imperative not only to *have* insurance coverage but to be fully aware of its extent and its conditions. For rare books, art, and manuscripts, partial liability may be financially feasible because usually a section rather than a whole collection succumbs at one time to fire, theft, or vandalism. Unique items, if irretrievably damaged or gone, cannot be replaced, so their value is not easily established. Ensure that all policy prerequisites (that is, "coverage void if . . .") are met.

Lastly, but foremost in importance, plan and execute, in written detail, a carefully thought-through disaster plan. Familiarize staff with its location, content, and method of implementation. To facilitate claims, keep duplicate copies or discs of the collections' holdings and their values, and the plan itself, in a safe but accessible place *off-site.*

In the lean and recessionary 1990s, special collections are under fire from almost everywhere. To be good is no longer enough! Libraries must find broader relevance, expanded clientele, and new sources of funding. Emerging technologies need to be investigated and, if expedient and affordable, harnessed quickly and efficiently. Avoid the temptation to lurch prematurely into costly ad hoc solutions. To survive we must become even more innovative and creative with fewer resources so that we may not only be more effective but be perceived so. For the current administrator/curator of a special collection of children's books "to do more with less" recalls the apt idiom of the miller's daughter in Rumpelstiltskin who must somehow manage under threat of demise to spin the straw into gold before dawn (when it is then claimed by others) and learn to cope the next day with the burden of more straw and the demand for more gold.

8

Funding
Special
Collections

Karen Nelson Hoyle

A hanging mobile with delicately floating weights provides a simile for the funding of special collections. Small institutions are like small mobiles, while gigantic institutions are like large constructions. Some mobiles possess extraordinary shape while others are of a simple design. Whatever the size, the principles remain the same. The weights represent important components of funding special collections. For a special collection to achieve fund-raising success, six factors must be kept in balance. These factors are expounded by Henry A. Rosso, founding director of The Fund Raising School, a program of the Center on Philanthropy at Indiana University, Indianapolis. The factors are

1. dynamic functions
2. institutional readiness
3. markets
4. management
5. human resources
6. vehicles[1]

Dynamic Functions

To have a successful fund-raising program, the parties involved first need to agree on the dynamic functions, or purpose, of a special collection and the constituents to be served. A clear understanding of the place of the special collection in the mission of the larger library must be expressed. The mission may be tied to historical preservation of the best in children's literature or a representative sampling of children's books from each decade. Planners must establish priorities and make plans for success. Being too ambitious and failing is demoralizing, but remaining unambitious is no fun. Objectives must be realistic and shared.

A succinct case must be stated, with the purpose for the special collection and the fund-raising focus reduced to a single phrase or sentence. Brainstorming about what the special collection could be ten years from now helps to establish priorities now. Then the grand plan can be broken down in five-year and one-year increments, with a plan or "wish list" emanating from that. This can translate into goals and objectives and a thoughtful list of priorities and possibilities. Each must be converted into a dollar figure. Each high priority carries a price tag, and the total of these determines part of the fund-raising goal.

Priorities drive the plan. If possible, the institution will provide funds for all the priorities. These might include salaries, physical plant, overhead, equipment (from shelving to computers, photocopy machine, and microfilm reader), printing, postage, supplies, lectures, programs, conferences, exhibits, travel for field work, attendance at professional conferences, and fellowships for visiting researchers. However, limited institutional financial resources usually necessitate fund-raising. As Dwight F. Burlingame stated in an article on library fundraising, "Private support supplements tax support to create a degree of excellence that otherwise would not be possible."[2]

Once the needs are agreed upon and a budget amount assigned, planners must decide which components of a special collection are more suitable for the organization to finance. Other components may appeal to individual donors or foundations. Planners need to analyze the collection to determine what aspect is most familiar to the recipients of fund-raising materials. They must identify what is unique and best understood by the public. The May Massee Collection in Emporia, Kansas, for example, houses the Robert McCloskey original journals, dummies, and art for his children's books, such as the Caldecott Award-winning *Make Way for Ducklings*. A grant proposal that highlights this title with which the public is most familiar might heighten the response to the entire proposal.

Institutional Readiness

The institution must be involved with each aspect of the fund-raising effort. When people believe in the purpose of the special collection and are convinced that the request is reasonable and valid, fund-raising success is greatly improved. Ultimately, the staff or volunteer must ask for a donation or for help from another volunteer to acquire a gift for the special collection. If people believe in the cause of the special collection, they are more likely to respond favorably when asked by a peer.

Staffing, cataloging, and preservation may be identified as high priorities or important needs. Problems in building support might arise if agreement on priorities is not reached at an early stage. For instance, if staff is not convinced that preservation of the books is a priority, then they will find it hard to be enthusiastic about writing copy or welcoming visitors in to see what the fund-raising campaign is all about.

Typically, the triad of "players" are the director, staff, and volunteers. If the governing board or director fails to see the need for a special collection, the enterprise is doomed from the start. All concerned must agree on the greatest needs and the consequences of meeting those priorities. For example, one librarian confided that after a catalog of the special collection's holdings was published, there were so many researchers visiting and reference inquiries to be answered that it was impossible to find time to catalog the incoming books.

Markets

Fund-raisers must identify, analyze, and target potential sources of funding for special collections. Possible markets are individuals, corporations, foundations, the state and federal government, coordinating agencies, and associations. Individuals placed on a mailing list might include members of a local literary club, Friends of another library, alumni, subscribers, and members of a local or national professional teacher or library association. Some corporations encourage generosity to nonprofit institutions or programs by matching employees' individual donations. Minnesota Mining and Manufacturing (3M), for example, matches monetary gifts to the Children's Literature Research Collections at the University of Minnesota.

Preliminary work might include developing profiles of groups or individuals. Misjudging the potential donor group will lead to high costs in time and money. Grant applications should be approached with care.

When the markets are identified, volunteers from the targeted market must be enlisted to support the cause from within that group's ranks. For example, if rare books need to be acquired, literary clubs may be contacted for potential gift books or funding. Therefore, fund-raisers need to recruit members of key clubs who may be interested in the special collection. However, if current books need to be acquired, publishers may be invited to become donors.

Another example of the benefits derived from focusing on organizations that are most likely to support the fund-raising effort is that of the Cooperative Children's Book Center (CCBC) at the University of Wisconsin in Madison. The CCBC is primarily a book-examination center for state residents. Both the State Department of Education and the university's School of Education agreed to this purpose and therefore fund the CCBC. A process validated the needs of constituents—the state teachers, librarians in the field, and registered students. While the state and university provide salaries and space, publishers have a natural interest in supplying books for the constituents to read. Beyond that goal, the staff sought a forum for bringing authors to the campus to meet the constituents. The conference department at the university provides the practical expertise to run such a conference, and the collection staff formulates the intellectual content. A Friends group provides money for special projects, such as lectures and display cases.

Foundations tend to fund innovative projects one time only. Each foundation has a distinct profile, and its formal parameters for funding are outlined in a printed brochure or directory. Some foundations or agencies insist on matching the dollars from another source.

Just because a foundation is wealthy does not mean it's a prospect. Submitting a grant application with an incorrect focus to a foundation is most often a waste of time and energy. Perusing the *Foundation Directory* or visiting a foundation resource center in large cities could be the first step to finding a potential match. Indexes provide key words such as "library," "book arts," or the name of the city and state. These terms should correlate with the purpose or goal of the special collection projects. Successful grant applications result from a good match of the proposing institution and a foundation with logical connections. For example, the de Grummond Collection received the Ezra Jack Keats original materials; therefore, the Ezra Jack Keats Foundation funded "The Image of the Child" exhibit and catalog in 1991.

The history of a group's giving program in the recent past might indicate trends. Social needs of hungry children and homeless adults may preempt libraries, while issues of access and literacy preempt special collections within the library. Save additional time by sending letters of inquiry or telephoning to get a sense of possible fund-raising success.

A local foundation may respond to a need to assist local people, but the end result may benefit others. The F. R. Bigelow Foundation, for example, funded the publication *The Kerlan Collection Manuscripts and Illustrations*. The foundation board responded to the proposal that teachers, librarians, and parents in St. Paul would efficiently find the materials in the Kerlan Collection with a printed catalog, but the spin-off was that the same publication could be used nationally by researchers. Another example of the broad reach of foundation donations is that of the Ezra Jack Keats Foundation, established in New York by the deceased author-illustrator of *The Snowy Day, Peter's Chair,* and other books. The foundation provides a research fellowship at the de Grummond Collection at the University of Southern Mississippi in Hattiesburg and an author/illustrator fellowship at the Kerlan Collection at the University of Minnesota.

Wisconsin's CCBC is funded by the State Department of Public Instruction Division for Library Services and the University of Wisconsin through the School of Education, both located in Madison. The federal government supports some national and state programs via the National Endowment to the Humanities (NEH) and library and education grants. NEH awarded the de Grummond Collection a grant to process, provide access to, and conserve its collection of manuscripts and illustrations. Although the grant resulted in a great deal of work being accomplished, grant proposals such as this demand a great deal of time and effort to write and revise, to direct the project, and to report at the end. Some curators compare writing a grant proposal to writing a book.

Associations such as Delta Kappa Gamma and university alumni may provide funds for a specific project. However, the organization may not repeat the gift annually. Members tend to have enough diversity in their interests that the organization turns to other causes.

Management

Management of the fund-raising effort is critical. A financial goal should be realistic so that it can be met within a given time frame. Planning and timing of an effort may mean orchestration of gift announcements. For example, if there is a fund-raising campaign, perhaps only one of the big donations would be announced near the beginning to heighten the excitement, and others would be announced near the end of the campaign. An individual or committee should monitor the fund-raising effort so it is coordinated within a time frame.

Staff need to have budget surveillance. Funds should be spent according to the budget lines. For example, the supply budget cannot be used for staff salaries. If a grant application is successful, an auditor may appear at any moment to check on the use of the funds.

The director, the board and key volunteers, the staff, and the development personnel must monitor the fund-raising process in light of its goals and objectives. In addition, they must later evaluate the procedures, the successes, and the failures. This provides a sense of ownership.

Volunteers might meet for coffee early on the day they visit potential donors and gather again to compare notes. Adequate staff in the office is needed to process and acknowledge every incoming pledge and check. Gifts must be acknowledged in an appropriate way, ranging from honor rolls in a newsletter to a reception for donors to naming a room or building after a substantial donor.

Human Resources

Human resources include volunteers, leaders, trustees, and staff. Trustees expect to provide examples by donating substantial amounts, making suggestions of people to call on, and being available to visit potential donors. Staff, too, could donate generously in accordance with their financial ability or time. Friends groups also may participate in public relations and fund-raising. Individuals can spread the message and promote understanding about the special collection. In addition, some people donate money as a memorial or to celebrate anniversaries. Others may provide funds for publications, lectures, and exhibitions.

Communications skills are important. Plans must be in place for communicating with potential donors, for the preparation of brochures, and for personal visits. If staff is inadequate, hired consultants can crystallize thinking and produce well-written materials.

Only committed individuals should participate in personal visits. Limited understanding of fund-raising and of the contemplated projects can damage the endeavor. However, people can be motivated to learn and practice new skills. Staff and volunteers usually need orientation and intermittent training. A fund-raising consultant can give workshops, assign readings, and lead discussions of a book such as Fisher Howe's *The Board Member's Guide to Fund Raising*. Remember, also, that volunteers will feel more competent and comfortable at the end of the fund-raising campaign than at the beginning.

A variety of training aids are available to fund-raisers. For example, the Fund Raising School of the Indiana University Center on Philanthropy in Indianapolis offers short courses at several locations around the country, while the Center on Philanthropy offers an academic degree program. Furthermore, more than ten thousand individuals are members of the professional National Society of Fund Raising Executives (NSFRE).[3] In 1991 there were more than one hundred chapters throughout the United States.

Literature abounds in the field of fund-raising, available at many public and academic libraries. Among the most helpful for librarians are Victoria Steele and Stephen Elder's *Becoming a Fundraiser* and a book edited by Dwight Burlingame, *Library Fundraising: Models for Success,* that brings together a number of excellent essays.[4] These experienced fund-raisers address such issues as special events, annual funds, capital campaigns, and planned giving.

Vehicles

Methods of fund-raising include annual giving, direct mail, capital campaigns, big gifts, deferred gifts, and renewals. Select the means of soliciting, ranging from a low-effort direct-mail campaign to a time-consuming (but probably more successful) effort involving personal visits by peers. Ideally, everyone committed to the special collection should donate at least once a year.

Direct-mailing campaigns should be broad-based. Lists can be purchased or rented from other organizations, such as friends of libraries groups. The packet might include information about the special collection, a request for money, and a return envelope. Check with the post office for bulk-mail requirements.

A capital campaign involves raising money for purchasing equipment or funding a building. Obtaining the big, or special, gift involves developing profiles of the prospect (potential donor) and finding the right person to call on the prospect. Details of a planned or deferred gift are usually arranged by a well-informed development officer or person with legal or tax training. Whatever the means or level of giving, the staff and volunteers should ask again the next year so a gift can be renewed or repeated.

Some special collections programs are innovative in their projects. For example, endowment funds proved insufficient to finance the publication of *The May Massee Collection: Creative Publishing for Children 1923-1963: A Checklist;* therefore, the Emporia State University's Endowment Association provided a no-interest loan and book sales reimbursed the fund. Another example is a special collection that has a budget-line or a revolving fund for producing and selling publications and other products where the profits are returned to the fund.

Fund-raising, however, needs to move dramatically away from the library book sale, which Dwight Burlingame noted was still the norm in 1990.[5] There may be a place for selling greeting cards, posters, and duplicate books, but quite often hidden costs counteract any profit. Staff and volunteer time used to advertise, fill orders, and keep accounts, along with postage, storage space, and sales tax need to be weighed. Endowments may prove more profitable in the long run. For example, in 1976 the Friends of the Osborne and Lillian H. Smith Collections at Toronto Public Library launched a trust fund. The interest accrued provides the funding for special purchases, such as a picture-letter from Beatrix Potter to her father.

The six aspects of fund-raising work together for success, as do the weights of a well-balanced mobile. If one of these—dynamic functions, institutional readiness, markets, management, human resources, or vehicles—is lacking or weak, it will affect the whole. Success is still possible, but the size and arrangement of the other weights have to compensate. It's best to proceed with these considerations, each carrying its own weight to maintain the balance in funding special collections. Fund-raising will be more successful if it is based on the premise that the institution will support a special collection and that individuals will donate if the special collection can keep the six factors of fund-raising working effectively.

Notes

1. *The Fund Raising School Study Guide.* San Rafael, Calif.: Fund Raising School, 1986. The Fund Raising School of Indiana University Center on Philanthropy is located at 550 W. North St., Ste. 301, Indianapolis, IN 46202.
2. Dwight Burlingame, "Public Libraries and Fundraising: Not-So-Strange Bedfellows," *Library Journal* 115 (July 1990): 52.
3. The National Society of Fund Raising Executives can be contacted at 1101 King St., Ste. 3000, Alexandria, VA 22314.
4. Victoria Steele and Stephen Elder, *Becoming a Fundraiser: The Principles and Practices of Library Development,* Chicago: American Library Assoc., 1992; Dwight F. Burlingame, ed., *Library Fundraising: Models for Success,* Chicago: American Library Assoc., 1995.
5. Burlingame, "Public Libraries and Fundraising," 53.

Further Reading

Burlingame, Dwight. "Public Libraries and Fundraising: Not-So-Strange Bedfellows." *Library Journal* 115 (July 1990): 52–4.

———. *Library Fundraising: Models for Success.* Chicago: American Library Assoc., 1995.

Flanagan, Joan. *The Grass Roots Fundraising Book.* Chicago: Contemporary Books, 1982.

The Foundation Directory. New York: Foundation Center (Distributed by Columbia Univ. Pr.), 1960– .

Howe, Fisher. *The Board Member's Guide to Fund Raising: What Every Trustee Needs to Know about Raising Money.* San Francisco: Jossey-Bass, 1991.

Kurzig, Carol M. *Foundation Fundamentals: A Guide for Grantseekers.* New York: The Foundation Center, 1980.

Rosso, Henry A. *The Fund Raising School Study Guide.* San Rafael, Calif.: The Fund Raising School, 1986.

———. *Rosso on Fund Raising: Lessons from a Master's Lifetime Experience.* San Francisco: Jossey-Bass, 1996.

Seymour, Harold J. *Designs for Fund-Raising.* Ambler, Pa.: FRI, 1966.

Steele, Victoria, and Stephen D. Elder. *Becoming a Fundraiser: The Principles and Practices of Library Development.* Chicago: American Library Assoc., 1992.

9

Public Relations and Programming

Linda Murphy and
Mary Beth Dunhouse

The purpose of this chapter is to provide you with methods of promoting your collection to increase its visibility and to generate support that will make possible improved access, preservation, and collection development. As the staff person responsible for the collection, you will need to create an awareness that enhances it within an institutional environment where competing needs struggle within static funding levels. Your collection's growth, use, and very existence may well hinge on the publicity program you build in the local, national, and international children's literature communities.

The increase in juvenile book production, focus on literacy and reading, and integration of children's books in the classroom are indications that children's literature has received increased attention in the last decade. The legitimacy of children's literature as a field worthy of critical study is demonstrated by the number of writings from scholars in various fields.

The preservation issue has made librarians more aware of the importance of addressing the deteriorating collections built over the last century and ensuring they will be available to future generations. If your collection is unique or contains items not commonly held in other American libraries, you have a responsibility to the nation's intellectual heritage to preserve and provide access to your collection.

Potential donors will consider your collection's size, prestige, support, and evaluation by others in the field as well as your institution's overall ability to support its donated materials. You will need to provide programs, lectures, exhibits, and catalogs that attract donors, scholars, and researchers in the field.

Children's literature is a part of this country's social, moral, and intellectual fabric. Your efforts to promote your collection will create a public awareness of this relationship and provide a rationale for collection maintenance and support.

Knowing Your Collection

To build effective awareness and support for your collection you must know its strengths and weaknesses. For staff working with collections a variety of tasks may be involved: reference requests, cataloging, shelving, acquisitions, donations, preservation work, exhibit preparation, participation in programs, and creation of catalogs and bibliographies.

You can start by identifying your collection's characteristics that make it unique within your locality and beyond. Seek out staff members and locate documentation that can provide information on the collection's origin and development prior to your involvement with it. Existing shelflists and accession lists can guide your initial exploration in defining a collection identity.

Knowing your collection gives you credibility with your institution's administration, subject specialists in your institution, researchers, and potential donors. Researchers are far more likely to be repeat users if the staff in charge of a collection know the material and can provide valuable assistance when necessary. If a potential donor of either material or funding is brought in by the administration, you will be in a position to provide the kind of knowledge that may determine the outcome of the donation.

Children's literature collections have large audiences. In identifying your audience you can begin with the type of institution housing your collection: academic, public, special, or private. Identify patrons who use the library where the collection is housed or serviced. You will need to consider what policies that cover the collection limit or expand its user base. If it is part of a rare books department, only qualified users may be able to consult collection materials. You may find through contact with patrons or other methods that you have an untapped group of people who would use the collection if they knew more about it. Your knowledge of the collection will help identify other potential patrons or groups who could support the collection.

Goals and Objectives

The development of your goals and objectives should be uniquely tailored to your collection. The purpose in building awareness and support is to showcase the collection in the best possible way. Your work in this area must harmonize with institutional policies. You may want to plan goals in phased increments so the success or failure is not tied to one effort. The resources you can draw on will also play a part. Some of the suggestions in this chapter will require staffing beyond that of a single person.

You also need to be aware of opportunities that may present themselves. For example, the collection can be publicized as part of some other individual or group initiative.

Going over your plans with supervisors or department heads will ensure that all parties are in agreement with your plan of action. They will also be able to provide resources and other support as your plans develop.

Opportunities for Printed Publicity

You can publicize your collection and make potential users and contributors more aware of your holdings and services through a number of different ways. Some are time intensive, while others require more-extensive funding. You may want to combine several of the activities explained in the following sections to begin your publicity campaign.

Mailing Lists

One of the first activities that should take place in any effort to publicize the collection is to develop a mailing list. You can start with professional membership lists, publishers, Friends of the Library, etc. Persons interested in and those who avidly collect children's books should be included on your mailing list. Add individuals to the list as you think of them. You may want to develop separate mailing lists if you feel that certain individuals or groups should be notified for specific events.

If you enter the names into a personal computer database, you can generate mailing labels. Set up the database so that corrections, additions, and deletions can be done easily. Your institution's computer center may be able to generate a mailing list as needed. By coding the list by user type you can identify target groups for special occasions.

Brochures and Videos

If your budget will allow it, a handsome brochure can publicize your collection and be used in a variety of settings. A brochure can give a brief background of the collection and highlight its unique areas. It can tell the reader what policies govern patron access, photocopying, and photography, for example. Include the collection's hours and phone number. Display the brochure as a handout in exhibit or program areas or at various information points throughout your institution. You can take it to conferences and distribute it, mail it for purely informational purposes, or mail it along with reference replies.

A video production describing the collection's holdings and functions can be used in a similar manner to brochures and should include the same information. Include selected items that would visually highlight collection strengths. Make multiple copies and loan them to interested libraries. The tape could be run continuously in your own institution, providing the public with the basics of your collection.

Bibliographies

A bibliography can give interested patrons precise information about the titles held in the collection. How extensive you make it depends on the collection size and on the purpose of the bibliography. A bibliography may be based on an exhibit or program content involving the collection. You may choose to generate a bibliography of new acquisitions or donations at appropriate intervals. Like brochures, bibliographies can be designed to serve as handouts and mailers.

Catalogs

Catalogs require an extensive amount of preparation, time, and funding. Consider your reasons for producing a catalog. A major exhibition or program can certainly justify creating one. You will need an in-house graphics person or access to an outside agency to prepare it. A donor may wish to underwrite the cost of producing the catalog. It can be marketed for sale, which will place printed information about the collection in other institutions.

A bibliographic catalog is another possibility. With existing technologies it is possible to generate name, title, and subject catalogs in printed or microfiche formats that can be distributed to multiple in-house locations and an infinite number of outside places. If your collection does not receive a great many acquisitions on a yearly basis or is going to stay at its present size, a bibliographic catalog in book or microformat may be very worthwhile because it will not need to be constantly updated.

Placing your catalog records in a national utility is a means of publicizing the collection as well as providing access to specific titles. The Archives and Manuscripts MARC (Machine-Readable Cataloging) format allows collection-level records to be input on the national utilities. If you have nonmonographic material (correspondence, photographs, memorabilia), you can create a collection-level record that will provide access to your collection.

In-House Publications

Your own in-house organs or institutional publications are other avenues for providing publicity. Contact the editor or other staff person so you know what sort of information is needed. Depending on the type of coverage, it may be possible to include for publication everything from an exhibit announcement to an article on the collection.

Developing an in-house newsletter for distribution through your mailing list is relatively easy with the desktop publishing techniques now available for personal computers. A newsletter can highlight collection activities on a regular basis. It can be sent to Friends groups, mailing-list patrons, or known professional groups. Newsletter content could center around announcements or accounts of programs held by your collection, information articles or subject bibliographies, renovation or building expansion plans, recent or new service descriptions, obituaries, and staff members and their accomplishments. Many major American children's literature research collections, such as the de Grummond Collection and the Kerlan Collection, issue newsletters regularly. Send for samples of these established newsletters to get ideas for starting your own.

If you have an in-house publicity person, meet with this individual to see how the publicity office could help your public relations efforts. This person can let you know what information is needed for press releases and deadlines for in-house and outside publications. Informing such individuals of your publicity plans will help them support you through contact with groups or individuals interested in your collections.

Local Media

Newspapers can give your collection coverage far beyond its institutional boundaries. If you do not have a publicity staff person or press office, contact the newspapers yourself. Start by contacting a book editor. Check to see if children's books are reviewed on a regular basis in your area newspapers. Reviewers may not know about your collection but could use it for their research and reference needs. Do not overlook smaller weekly papers in your area in addition to any large dailies. Send an editor or reviewer information on a regular basis to keep your collection in the forefront of their considerations for a feature. Send in your collection-related events to be included in newspaper listings of current events and exhibits.

Public broadcasting stations or local television and radio stations often provide free air time for public service messages. Take advantage of this to make announcements of programs, exhibits, and speakers via these media. Also, look for programs featuring children's book talks, storytelling, or informational presentations about local institutions in which to participate. A more-direct approach would be to design your own program directed to a specific audience.

In large institutions the public relations officer is most likely responsible for writing press releases. If you are responsible for writing your own press releases, remember the following guidelines.

- Word process or type all communications. Double space the text and triple space between paragraphs using only one side of the paper.
- Include your library's name on the press release.
- Cite the full name of the children's literature collection.
- Center the title of the press release in caps at the top of the page.
- Outline the who, what, when, where of the story in the first paragraph.

- Keep the paragraphs short and use a consistent style.
- Provide a release date, the name of a contact person, and a phone number.
- Have a colleague proofread the release before you send it.
- Keep the original for your file and send copies.

Journals

Announcements to appropriate journals will let others know what is happening with your collection. Depending on the journal, you can send in announcements of upcoming exhibits, special acquisitions, and programs. Include information about the availability of a catalog or bibliography. You might also prepare an article or a special feature on the collection and submit it. Check *Professional Periodicals in Children's Literature* for possible contacts.

Internet/World Wide Web Opportunities for Publicity

The Internet/World Wide Web offers a number of possibilities for publicizing your collection and its holdings. The widespread access to the Internet through home computers means that potential users such as researchers, donors, publishers, authors, illustrators, and others will be able to learn about your collection through a myriad of avenues.

Your own library's Web page is a good place to start sending out information about your collection, its holdings, hours and rules of use, exhibits, special events, bibliographies, available publications, etc.

Depending on the size of your institution, you may be able to prepare the information on a word processing program and make it available to your system's librarian or other staff for input to the library's home page. If not, you may be able to call on patrons with expertise in the design of Web pages, or you may want to use a local firm that specializes in Web page design and content.

The availability of help both on-line and in your community should aid in the creation of a well-designed Web page. Look at the Web pages of other libraries, particularly those with special collections in children's literature, and consider adopting features that are applicable to your collection. Try moving around the Web pages and related links, noting what seems to facilitate access to the collection. Often library Web pages provide links to other Web sites with related information. You will have to decide if you want to include other links or aim for a self-contained page.

The one constant of the Web is its fluid nature. Maintain your Web page so that the information on it remains current. Start by examining an existing brochure and noting those features you want to include such as hours the collection is open, location, address (mail, fax, E-mail), collection use, basic and more-specific descriptions, and links to your local catalog. Additional features include special exhibits, events, publications, and announcements. Consider if you will take reference questions by providing an E-mail address at your site. Include the conditions, if any, under which you will loan material for exhibit or allow photocopying or photographs of collection items.

Graphic material such as illustrations from your collection can enhance your Web site and make it more than a page of solid text. Graphics break up the information and make it easier for the reader to assimilate the specifics of your collection. Illustrations can highlight the illustrators represented in your collection. Be sure to use only those graphics that are out of copyright or to which your library holds the copyright. Keep in mind that the display of graphic information on some computers is very time consuming to load. Some Internet providers have a feature that allows the user to load the information without the graphics. The basics of your collection should be in a meaningful text so that users looking at your pages without the graphics will still get the information they need.

You may be familiar with the HTML (HyperText Markup Language), which is used on the Web. If you are already acquainted with HTML, you may see possibilities in the creation of your Web page. Library school students, Web-page designers, and local computer people may be able to help you by doing the actual coding. Computer magazines, publications, and workshops are also available to explain these languages and their use.

Linking to Other Sites

In your explorations on the Web you may have found sites that contain listings and descriptions of special collections in children's literature. Instructions are given for sending your collection's description for inclusion at these sites. You may want to provide links to these sites from your Web page. More specifically, you can link to the specific Web pages of authors and illustrators. For example, if you are strong in editions of *Alice in Wonderland,* you could search for sites that feature the Alice titles or Lewis Carroll. How far you wish to go with this will depend on your own energy and resources or whether you can assign staff to this effort. Potentially you could link to hundreds of sites, but many may provide little or no worthy information to a user. The usefulness of a site depends primarily on how well it is maintained. If you decide to link to other sites, develop a plan for periodically checking those sites to ensure that you are not sending people to nonfunctioning or outdated sites.

Evaluation

Test your site and be prepared to change information, location, and links that don't seem to be working. Try to have colleagues and patrons use the page and give you feedback on what they find useful as well as what could be revised. Web pages often include an E-mail address so that users can respond with questions or comments on the site.

Person-to-Person Opportunities

It is also possible to promote the collection on a person-to-person basis. Opportunities to meet and talk with like-minded individuals can be found in your own institution, at a local or state-level meeting, or even at an international conference.

Professional Associations

Professional associations will give you a network of contacts of other librarians working with special children's literature collections. You will be able to share information that can lead to increased publicity for your collection. Publications generated by the association may give you an opportunity to include information on your collection. Professional association meetings that include exhibitors will give you contact with publishers who may be producing guides and directories of special collections of children's books.

Library and subject-related conferences and workshops on the local, regional, and national level provide other opportunities for publicizing the collection. In fact, you may be invited or volunteer to speak on the collection. Contact the program sponsor to see if collection brochures can be included in the program handouts or placed on tables in a meeting or reception area. You may also be able to announce a collection event or publication at these meetings.

Collectors

Certainly collectors of children's books will be interested in your collection's scope and may use it as they research their own collecting activities. Since you both are working in an area of mutual interest, collectors are good contacts. They may be able to support some of your publicity efforts. They will also be able to put other collectors in touch with you. Collectors sometimes have newsletters that might provide another option for publicity, or they may have interest groups who tour institutional collections or attend programs.

Publishers

With publishers, the contact can be of mutual benefit. Their awareness of your collection can result in programs, reference use, exhibit supplements, and possibly new children's books. Contact with the children's book editor or library marketing director will help them become aware of your collection as a reference source. You may be able to invite editors, authors, and illustrators to participate in a program because of an already established relationship. They may provide posters, bookmarks, and author biographical information for a program or exhibit. It never hurts to send a publisher notification of an event including or featuring its authors or illustrators. Again, like local authors, local publishers should be included in your publicity efforts.

Booksellers and Dealers

Book dealers can help in a number of ways. Through advance arrangement, they may be able to bring in multiple copies of an author's or illustrator's works for a special program or a flyer to include in a packet of material you will be distributing. Dealers can alert you to material that you may be interested in purchasing, and they can put you on the mailing list for catalogs they produce. Their awareness of your collection and the type of items you are looking for can put you in touch with other dealers. Dealers with commercial space may be willing to post flyers or other announcements for your collection. For your own reference and referral purposes, it is a good idea to maintain a list of local book dealers who either specialize in or stock children's books.

Academic Institutions

If your setting is near or part of an academic institution, you are probably aware of those departments that lend themselves to publicity efforts because of their ties to children's literature. Review your academic catalog or directory by department; you may come up with some surprising inclusions. Science departments are natural inclusions with the increasing focus on teaching these subjects in elementary and secondary education. Current and future teachers in these fields should be made aware of the trade children's literature that is available. Scientific illustrations are areas of research that your collection may be able to support. Your institution's education department should also be made aware of the collection. Children's literature can be the basis for a special relationship between your collection and the English department. If children's literature is taught within this department, you can prepare material that will lead the teacher and students into your collection. Art teachers looking for illustration examples will be able to use your collection.

Continuing education has possibilities as well. Examine existing courses and determine if your collection can be incorporated into course contents. In fact, you may see a possibility for a course *you* could design and teach that would use your collection.

Library schools are another natural tie. You can offer access to your collection to provide additional depth. Your collection should also be a source of reference for children's services courses.

For any contact with these departments, meet with appropriate faculty. Try to determine if their needs and your needs match. Explore different approaches, such as class or site visits.

Local Authors and Illustrators

Local authors and illustrators can be an enormous boon to the awareness of your collection within the community. These individuals can be brought in for programs that focus attention on their works and your collection. A local chapter of an interest group, such as the Society of Children's Book Writers and Illustrators, may be interested in what your collection has to offer. If your collection includes original materials or presentation copies, you may be contacted by a local writer or illustrator about a possible donation.

Donors

In dealing with donors, it helps to have an institutional policy already in place. Donors are looking for an institution that will house, publicize, and make available their material for the life of the collection. You and your institution need to be clear on what donor conditions can be met. Your institution's history of donor relationships will influence who approaches you. Certainly, donations of significant materials will publicize your collection and lead other donors to your door. You are in a stronger position to receive donations if you can demonstrate the strength, importance, and uniqueness of the existing collection. You need to show how the donation will enhance already developed collection strengths and to show that you can support research in the subject aspect of the donation. Donors may very well ask about what publicity you can provide for their material.

Donated materials may need special care and handling beyond what the rest of the collection requires. If the donor has asked for and received guarantees of special consideration in these areas, the institution will have to provide it. If it is material that your public will begin asking for, it will need to be made available, which will place additional demands on your institution. In addition to institutional support, a donor may want to provide financial support for his or her donated collection.

Internal Contacts

Consider specific departments or individuals within your own institution who would like to know about the collection or who in your opinion should know more about the collection. These in-house staff members can become strong supporters if you are working in interdepartmental areas, and they will think of the collection when planning cooperative programs. Increased patronage of the collection can result because you have made the effort to inform such individuals, and they will, in turn, put other people in contact with you.

In-House Programs

In-house programs give you the opportunity to showcase the collection on its own ground. You can determine and control the program components to your advantage. If your institution has a good physical setup, programming will be that much easier.

Plan programs months in advance of the event. Timing is important; the season, the month, the day of the week, and the time of day can enhance or detract from audience attendance and interest. A survey of other children's literature events in your area can provide information for designing a calendar of optimal program dates. Develop a checklist of audience expectations, program design and goals, outside coordination considerations, impact on staff, and projected costs. At the completion of the event, review the objectives to see if they were met.

Define the relationship between your collection and your program goals. You may want to try planning several different types of programs to test which ones work best to fulfill your goals.

The possibilities are endless depending on your goals and resources: an evening program of one to two hours with a reception afterward, an all-day or a half-day program, etc. For day-long programs it is helpful to give the audience a break in the form of various sessions. Alternate more formally structured sessions with an informal group discussion. Give the audience a chance to meet and interact with each other.

The beauty of in-house programs means you can call on your colleagues and have institutional support. You will have to see that the physical space is prepared for the program: the house cleaning is complete and the chairs, program signs, flowers, and necessary audiovisual equipment are in place. Ask permission from the program speakers to audio or videotape. Make sure that in-house staff supporting your event are invited and acknowledged during the program. Remember, even if you are the one who conceptualized the program, its success or failure can also hinge on your colleagues' involvement.

Existing brochures and other materials to hand out or a bibliography prepared specifically for the program will remind program attendees of your collection. An exhibit related to the program may be a possibility. Bibliographies and exhibitions provide attendees with a visual or written reference to works in your collection. Provide opportunities to visit the collection during a lunch break or reception.

Speakers

Programs can be developed around your collection's focus. Local authors or illustrators are often willing to present programs. By using local talent you create a positive name regionally for your collection and institution. Tell the potential speaker whether you can pay an honorarium or simply cover expenses. At the least, expect to pay for local transportation and provide an excellent lunch or dinner. Contact speakers through their publishers or look in local directories compiled by booksellers or writers' groups. For example, the New England Children's Booksellers' Association publishes the *Directory of New England Authors and Illustrators of Children's Books* listing names, addresses, publishers, and speaking fees.

Involve other groups in program planning if institutional policy allows. So that you and your small staff are not overwhelmed, see if professional organizations or other institutions will support you. In exchange for cosponsorship, they will bring promotional materials and can speak briefly on their organization during your program.

Identifying your audience is particularly important. You need to determine if you will be able to logistically handle the expected number of people, so take care not to overbook your audience. Review the transportation and location factors and information on local transportation, maps, and possibly lodgings and restaurants.

From publishing contacts you may learn that an author or illustrator will be visiting your city as part of a cross-country speaking tour. This is particularly valuable for writers and illustrators from outside the United States whose travel expenses, if paid locally, might prohibit such a visit. These preplanned speaking engagements are set up to highlight the speaker and his or her works, not to provide you with a custom-made program of your choosing. As long as both parties know what the intent is, you mutually benefit. Unless the publisher is looking for some other platform, a library is an ideal place to feature a children's author. Find out from the publisher's representative the type of audience, its size, and whether autographs will be permitted. Depending on the program time, and in consultation with the publisher, a lunch, dinner, or reception may round out the program.

The advantages are many in having a preplanned program brought to your institution: You can provide material on your collection. In addition, you will have made contact with a publisher, author, or illustrator who, if comfortable with this engagement, will consider your institution for future ones. The program will bring in other children's literature people in your area who may approach you about joint program proposals. Also, the speaker may request information on your collection. Furthermore, it is possible your collection will receive a donation of materials. Most importantly, with a prepackaged program you have to do some of the work but you do not have to plan the program's content or take care of the speaker every minute.

Panel discussions provide a program with contrasting viewpoints and can more readily involve the audience. Speakers can give a short presentation followed by questions from a moderator and the audience. Always allow time for questions, and if possible, a more-informal setting for further contact between the speakers and audience.

Tours

Tours are a wonderful way to introduce your collection to an individual or a group. In planning, consider the security of the material and the tour's impact on staff and patrons. Think about whether a general tour will suit each group or whether some individual tailoring should be provided.

Tours are the best kind of "show and tell" because the audience is physically located in the collection. It is easy for you to look up authors, titles, or subjects in your catalog, pull material, display it, and talk about it. The resources offered in the collection are immediately apparent. If your area offers other children's literature-related attractions you can design a self-guided tour with instructions on how to get to the bookstore, historic author's home, library, etc.

Collection Presentations

Contact with children's literature people in your local, regional, and national organizations can lead to speaking invitations from them. This is your chance to focus solely on your presentation while someone else worries about the complete event. As you plan your presentation, you should consider which subject you are expected to talk about, within what time frame, the number of other speakers, and audience size. Determine what aspect of your collection will have meaning for the audience in terms of the group's goals, concerns, plans, needs, and interests. Your brochures and handouts can be distributed as part of your presentation. Let the program coordinator know if you are going to need audiovisual equipment. A slide show accompanying your narration will give the audience a visual presentation of your collection; hands-on exhibit items can be passed around for examination. The enthusiastic sharing of your collection's unique qualities will stay with your audience and create a climate for future reference and contacts.

Exhibits and Receptions

In-House Exhibits

Research collections, which may have limited patron access, can be promoted with in-house exhibits. Exhibitions present an opportunity to bring supporters into the library for opening receptions or programs related to the exhibit topic. Collection managers should be prepared to offer formal or informal exhibition tours. This is an important method of developing new support for your special collection.

Your collection's holdings are the springboard for exciting topical or visual themes for children's book exhibitions. A calendar of significant dates within the fields of the history of children's literature or the development of children's book illustration and book design or a directory of both contemporary and retrospective regional authors and artists can provide a structure from which you can develop exhibition themes. Keep in mind that the exhibition should communicate something meaningful and should not depend too heavily on the written word; it should present a visual message.

Well-prepared exhibitions are time consuming to organize. Showings should be planned to last at least one month to ensure a return on the preparation time invested.

Your powers of creativity will be called upon in any exhibit design, particularly if the exhibit space is less than ideal. Successful book display should incorporate normal reading conditions. The print should be viewed at a correct angle and distance to be read. An ideal presentation for books would be in secure flat cases with a slight incline of not more than ten degrees from a horizontal position. Prevent books from slipping by using book props that support the entire back of the book or placing books on an adjustable plastic ledge or holder that can be screw-mounted to the base of the display case. Avoid any strain on the book's binding. Show books open or closed; in fact, a variety of angles can add visual interest to the exhibition. Open books need to have retaining straps made of nonalkaline plastic. Such strips loop around the volume pages, are cut to match the book's size, and are held together by double-faced tape. Depending on the length of the exhibition and the condition of the books on display, periodically you may need to open books to other pages or to close a book to reduce strain on the binding.

Fit fluorescent light bulbs with ultraviolet filters. Position lighting in the case to allow for a clear view with no glare. Check with your preservation officer or regional conservation specialist on appropriate light and humidity levels for your exhibit cases.

Case backgrounds should be neutral in color, have a minimum of texture, and be free of substances that could cause a chemical change. Clear bibliographic identification of each item on display is essential. If the display area is physically removed from the collection, indicate on each label the title of the collection from which the items on display originate.

A specially designed exhibition title sign, prominently positioned in each display case, provides a visual continuum connecting cases for the patron. If backed with colored paper, these signs can add a little zip to case design. Clip art or reproduced illustrations from the public domain, such as those available from Dover Publications, can sometimes be used successfully in exhibits.

It is always a good idea to compile a bibliography or checklist of works displayed in an exhibition. If a finished product cannot be produced, a rough list should be available for in-house use to document your efforts and to refer to in the event patrons want to know which titles were exhibited once the show has ended. An exhibition catalog or bibliography prepared for free distribution during the exhibition is a strong promotional tool. Besides advertising the collection's name and providing a permanent record of a selected segment of the collection's holdings, either can serve as a reference for the patron's further research. Phone numbers and persons to contact for further information are crucial pieces of information to include on any handouts. It is useful to keep research materials used for the exhibition's preparation available for quick consultation during the display period.

Joint Exhibits

A joint exhibit is another way to highlight your collection as part of a show that brings in items from several other areas. It can mean that you set up your own cases to bring out a particular aspect of the theme within a larger display. A show designed like this will give your collection exposure and broaden its awareness beyond children's literature groups.

One area to consider before becoming involved in a joint exhibit of material is the rationale for the exhibition and the connection of the private material to your own collection. There should be a balance between the materials exhibited. Publicity efforts should not focus on the private material at the expense of your collection's holdings.

A joint exhibit will provide contact with other in-house staff or with the outside group working with you. Each may be able to put you in touch with other groups and individuals.

Loans to Other Institutions

Loaning your collection's items to another institution for an exhibit is another option, providing certain conditions are met. First you need to determine whether institutional policy allows loans.

Other factors to consider include the condition of items and the impact the loan will have on the collection. Assess the long-term impact on the collection in the event of loss or damage. If the item cannot be loaned, a substitution may be possible.

Along with your in-house considerations you should receive or ask for the following information from the requesting institution before making a commitment:

> exhibit title, focus, and time frame
> description of the display of the item
> lighting
> environment
> security measures
> insurance responsibilities, if any
> conditions of transport

In addition, your collection's name and institution should be given in the exhibit and on all citations to the item.

Directories and National Utilities

Try to familiarize yourself with secondary sources citing children's literature collections or special collections. Significant directories that list collections of children's literature are *Directory of Special Libraries and Information Centers* by Brigitte T. Darnay and Janice A.

DeMaggio, the third edition of *Special Collections in Children's Literature* by Dolores Blythe Jones, and *Subject Collections: A Guide to Special Book Collections and Subject Emphases* by Lee Ash and William G. Miller. If your collection is not now cited in a directory, write to the publisher requesting notification for inclusion in the next edition. There is a possibility that the publishers have sent the questionnaires in the past, but they may have been directed to the wrong department of your institution. Make sure all employees know about your collection so that questionnaires and surveys can be forwarded to you for completion. Also be aware of new reference sources, especially if the editors are now trying to contact institutions for needed information.

Professional associations also send out questionnaires that may relate to your collection. Remind library directors to contact you for your input to the appropriate section.

Entering your catalog records in one of the national utilities is another means for making users and librarians in other parts of the country aware of the collection. It may help when preparing grants to be able to cite this fact. You can include this in your promotional materials as well.

Further Reading

Ash, Lee, and William G. Miller, with the collaboration of Barry Scott, Kathleen Vickery, and Beverly McDonough. *Subject Collections: A Guide to Special Book Collections and Subject Emphases as Reported by University, College, Public, and Special Libraries and Museums in the United States and Canada.* 2 vols. 7th ed. New Providence, N.J.: R. R. Bowker Co., 1993.

Blake, Barbara Radke, and Barbara L. Stein. *Creating Newsletters, Brochures, and Pamphlets: A How-To-Do-It Manual.* New York: Neal-Schuman, 1992.

Darnay, Brigitte T., and Janice A. DeMaggio, eds. *Directory of Special Libraries and Information Centers.* 3 vols. 14th ed. Detroit: Gale, 1991.

Dolnick, Sandy. *Friends of Libraries Sourcebook.* 3d ed. Chicago: American Library Assoc., 1996.

Edsall, Marian S. *Library Promotion Handbook.* Phoenix, Ariz.: Oryx, 1980.

Hall, Margaret. *On Display: Design Grammar for Museum Exhibitions.* 2d rev. ed. London: Lund Humphries, 1992.

Jones, Dolores Blythe. *Special Collections in Children's Literature: An International Directory.* 3d ed. Chicago: American Library Assoc., 1995.

Karp, Rachelle S., ed. *Part-Time Public Relations with Full-Time Results: A PR Primer for Libraries.* Chicago: Publications Committee of the Public Relations Section, Library Administration and Management Association, American Library Assoc., 1995.

Kies, Cosette. *Marketing and Public Relations for Libraries.* Metuchen, N.J.: Scarecrow, 1987.

Leerburger, Benedict A. *Promoting and Marketing the Library.* rev. ed. Boston: G. K. Hall, 1989.

Reetz, Marianne, comp. *Professional Periodicals in International Children's Literature: A Guide.* 3d rev. ed. Munich: International Youth Library, 1994.

Roberts, Anne F., and Susan Griswold Blandy. *Public Relations for Libraries.* Englewood, Colo.: Libraries Unlimited, 1989.

Schaeffer, Mark. *Library Displays Handbook.* New York: H. W. Wilson, 1991.

Seager, Andrew J., Sarah J. Roberts, and Carol Z. Lincoln. *Check This Out: Library Program Models.* Washington, D.C.: Office of Educational Research and Improvement, U.S. Dept. of Education, 1987.

Sherman, Steve. *ABC's of Library Promotion.* 3d ed. Metuchen, N.J.: Scarecrow, 1992.

Walters, Suzanne. *Marketing: A How-to-Do-It Manual for Librarians.* New York: Neal-Schuman, 1992.

10

Friends Groups

Serenna F. Day

You may be working with an established special collection or merely in the planning stages of starting one, but you'll always do better, as the old Beatles song suggests, "with a little help from your friends." They may be called Friends, Support Groups, Circles, or Boosters, but from the glittering white-tie galas at the country's largest art museums to the bake sales at the local school, educational and cultural institutions have long benefited from the efforts of these dedicated volunteers.

Advantages of Having a Friends Group

There are many good reasons for having a Friends group. The first that comes to mind is monetary support. Crass, but true. Friends are able to solicit funds for your collection when institutional policies do not permit staff to do so. Friends can raise money through public events that give members a chance to demonstrate their creative and organizational skills. Nothing fires up a group more than planning such events. The enthusiasm and decibel levels rise as they work out details. You have an important role in all of this, which will be discussed later.

Friends of Children and Literature (FOCAL) is the support group of the children`s literature department of the Los Angeles Public Library. FOCAL's main objectives are to raise money to provide funds for outreach activities of the department as well as to promote and enhance its special collections and areas of strength in the general collection. Members also volunteer time to assist with the collections.

Highlights of the Los Angeles Public Library's children's literature department include a Mother Goose collection of approximately 1,000 titles (as yet uncataloged), a rich and varied international languages book collection representing juvenile literature published in more than 50 countries, and a doll collection of 450 dolls from countries throughout the world. A recent acquisition is the Gladys English Collection of Original Art from Children's Books, an important group of paintings and drawings donated in memory of a former coordinator of children's services at Los Angeles Public Library. FOCAL has held a series of theater parties to raise money to restore and frame these fragile works.

Just as Friends can solicit cash donations, they can also seek gifts for the collection. Staff activity in this area may be construed as self-serving, but Friends feel no such inhibitions. Also, busy and active supporters frequently belong to other organizations with similar educational or cultural goals, and this network can help to optimize your opportunities for reaching prospective donors of gifts or bequests. For example, enthusiastic members of FOCAL have recently solicited gifts to the doll collection from such far-flung countries as Armenia, Thailand, Zimbabwe, and New Zealand.

Friends provide a loyal constituency. They can champion your cause by speaking directly to civic leaders or other power bases in the community because they are not bound by the chain of command. Your administration will also appreciate this support. At budget time friends can lobby for funding for specific activities or library collections. FOCAL Board members spoke before the Budget Committee of the Los Angeles City Council in support of library services for children. Their appeal helped to reduce cuts in book budgets and service hours and increased public awareness of the department's collection strengths and outreach activities.

Another positive result of this support is improved staff morale. Employees take more pride in the collection and their work in the library as they see the benefits of the Friends' activities. Members of a Friends group frequently volunteer to assist in the day-to-day functions of special collections. One FOCAL member has spent hundreds of hours researching and cataloging the doll collection. Another has begun to index the numerous varieties of books in the international languages book collection to provide access to such items as alphabet books and unique illustrations.

If you expect the administration and the public to appreciate your collection(s), you need to publicize its value to them. Friends can help to promote the collections in a number of ways: They can issue newsletters and other publications to help spread the word. FOCAL publishes a quarterly newsletter to publicize the group's activities and library news. Members help mount displays and prepare booklets and brochures featuring the many strengths of the department. Long-range plans of FOCAL include the publication of a catalog of the Mother Goose collection.

But, most of all, your Friends will provide credibility for your special collections. The administration of your institution will view the collection as worthy of volunteer effort and, therefore, worthy of support and maintenance. An example of this support was the decision of the Los Angeles Public Library to designate annual funding for additions to the Gladys English Collection. Due to the Friends' many activities, programs, and publications that provided visibility and promoted the uses of the collection, professional colleagues as well as the general public perceived the collection as a valuable addition to the community.

In addition to working with special collections, FOCAL publicizes the department's extensive and important collection of California materials through its annual FOCAL Award, given to a creative work that enriches a child's appreciation for and understanding of California. FOCAL also focuses attention on the importance of children's literature by annually honoring a local author or illustrator for his or her body of work as well as for his or her contributions to the school and library communities. This constitutes a lifetime achievement award, complete with official government proclamations, tributes from children, congratulatory telegrams and letters, and a scrapbook of the entire event.

What Friends Have Done

The success of FOCAL did not go unnoticed by other departments of the Los Angeles Central Library, which soon founded its own Friends groups. There are now a total of six support groups at Central—groups that often cooperate on monthly used book sales and work together on major library events such as author readings and receptions.

Of course, "umbrella" Friends groups and foundations of public libraries and educational institutions can be tremendously supportive. For example, the Foundation of the Boston Public Library provides funding for acquisitions as well as providing exhibition expenses for the rare book department and the Alice M. Jordan Collection, a rich, worldwide selection of children's literature. The San Francisco Public Library's Friends group has cooperated with the Women's National Book Association to provide an endowment for an annual symposium celebrating the Effie Lee Morris Collection.

A good example of the efficacy and fine work of a Friends group is demonstrated by the work of the Friends of the Kerlan Collection at the University of Minnesota. This collection of more than 60,000 children's books dating from the 1700s to the present also includes manuscript and source materials. The active Friends group fulfills its goals of promoting the importance and uses of the collection through many activities. It prepares portfolios and teacher guide kits for use in schools; selects, prints, and markets note cards using illustrations from the collection; sponsors programs featuring experts in the field of children's literature; publishes a newsletter; and selects the annual Kerlan Award recipient and sponsors the award banquet.

Starting a Friends Group

Once you are convinced that a Friends group is desirable, your next step is to convince your supervisors and to obtain administrative approval. This approval will be forthcoming when they learn that there is little or no cost involved other than postage and a few flyers. In these days of tight budgets, administrators welcome the opportunity to attract and use volunteers.

Prepare a list of projects and activities with which the Friends can assist and mention that members of your community have already expressed interest in such a group. Of course, this will require advance planning on your part in contacting representative individuals from your service community. A public library, for example, will want to involve people from the local school systems, parents, and loyal patrons as well as people in related fields such as bookstore owners and teachers of children's literature at nearby colleges or universities. Once you have made your community contacts, and gained approval to proceed, what is the next step?

Do it! After creating a list of benefits to other institutions and the general community, meet with a small core group of involved enthusiasts. A small group of a dozen or fewer members will result in more-efficient discussions and more accomplishments. Ask each group member to bring a list of ten or fifteen people who are very likely to join and who would be motivated to participate. Tell this core group that you are looking for a few leaders, either from this group or from their lists. Brainstorm about the goals and activities of a Friends group, taking notes for the benefit of the bylaws committee.

Use news releases and flyers to attract others, and invite the people on your mailing list to an organizational meeting. At that meeting, elect a small slate of officers and appoint a bylaws committee. Keep the bylaws simple and have written goals and a formal, but not too rigid, structure. If your bylaws provide for standing and ad hoc committees as well as presidential board appointments, you can avoid frequent amendments.

Before you begin, be sure to write to the Friends of Libraries USA (FOLUSA) for a packet of valuable ideas on forming a Friends organization. This packet includes information on how to gain tax-exempt status, a step that should be completed as soon as possible. Important information can also be obtained at FOLUSA's Web page at http://www.folusa.com/. Many states also have Friends group consortiums. Addresses are available from your state library association. Many statewide groups also have a presence on the Web. For example, the Friends of California Libraries has a very informative site at http://www.friendcalib.org/.

These initial planning stages call for critical and delicate dealings. You must, like Janus, face in both directions. While encouraging and inspiring your new Friends, you must make them aware of the institution's goals and policies. Most importantly, you must keep your administration informed. Tact and diplomacy are required to guide your fledgling group. A compatible board is essential, but you must be alert to the formation of cliques or the appearance of favoritism as appointments are made. Remember those diverse segments of your service community? You want as many of them as possible represented on your Friends board.

Sustaining Your Friends Group

Congratulations! You did it. You founded your Friends group. The initial hard work may be over, but you need to maintain your good work as liaison. You are the bond between these two very different entities, your Friends and your institution. Be goal oriented. Friends activities should relate to the goals and requirements of the institution. When your Friends meet, remember that it is their club and although you want them to exercise their enthusiasm and individuality, it is your job to keep them on track. For example, it may be a worthy and exciting project to donate a new swing set to the local playground, but it is beyond the scope of the mission of your Friends group. Their pursuits should promote and enhance the collection and activities of your library.

You may also need to serve as a balance for overambitious planning. Suggest one or two well-advertised annual events instead of many energy-diluting smaller ones. Be sure that each new activity involves different people so that the same few members don't carry the whole load.

Programs are the life-blood of most Friends groups, but remind the group of the five *P*s of every successful program:

1. *Plan.* Start early and make a written list of each task, assigning responsibility and a completion date.
2. *Promote.* Involve the general membership, not just the board, so that everyone feels a sense of commitment.
3. *Publicize.* This includes everything from flyers to the news media, from word of mouth to something truly attention-getting, like street banners or a float in a local parade.
4. *Perspire.* Impress on the committee that workers *work* during the exhibit, luncheon, or symposium so that the attendees can enjoy it.
5. *Preen.* Everyone can do this as they review a successful event.

Even success cannot be taken for granted. It is up to you to continually assess the progress of the Friends. Are they expending their energies on too many activities that do not enhance or promote the stated goals of the group? Are they merely having meetings and not gaining new members or producing results? Is the board stagnant? Maybe it's time to try a new venture or to recruit new segments of the community. Perhaps it would be advantageous to form an alliance with another organization on a joint project that is beneficial to both groups. For example, one year the Central Library Docents, who conduct tours of the building, sponsored an essay contest to provide free tickets to a few local children and their parents for the annual FOCAL Awards luncheon. The activity resulted in new members for both groups.

Whatever you plan, remember your Friends' original goals. Your role is to interpret your institution's position so that both can enjoy satisfaction and success. There's a lot of fun in all of this, as well as a sense of accomplishment, but the real reward for you and your staff is when your Friends become your friends. Go for it!

CONTRIBUTORS

Mary E. Bogan has been the special collections librarian and children's literature specialist at the William Allen White Library at Emporia State University since 1976. She was a member of the Kansas Library Network Board Preservation Advisory Council that helped the KLNB Preservation Committee develop a 1993 preservation plan for Kansas. She has also presented workshops on basic preservation.

Serenna F. Day was senior librarian in the Children's Literature Department of the Los Angeles Public Library for eighteen years until her retirement. She is the editor of the *Horn Book Index* (Oryx Press, 1990).

Mary Beth Dunhouse is coordinator of special projects and collections at the Boston Public Library. She compiled the *International Directory of Children's Literature* (Facts On File, 1986) and contributed to *Teaching Children's Literature: Issues, Pedagogy, Resources* (Modern Language Association, 1992).

Karen Nelson Hoyle is professor and curator of the Children's Literature Research Collections at the University of Minnesota Libraries. She has served as president of the Children's Literature Association and is the author of *Wanda Gag* (Twayne, 1994).

Dolores Blythe Jones is curator of the de Grummond Children's Literature Collection at the University of Southern Mississippi, a position she has held since 1986. She is the editor of *Special Collections in Children's Literature: An International Directory* (ALA, 1995) and *Children's Literature Awards and Winners* (Gale Research, 1994, 3d ed.).

The late **John M. Kelly** served as curator of the de Grummond Children's Literature Collection from 1978 to 1986, when he assumed the position of university bibliographer, also at the University of Southern Mississippi. At the time of his death in 1994 he was the chief bibliographer for the University Libraries at the University of Alabama.

Anne Lundin is an assistant professor on the faculty of the University of Wisconsin–Madison School of Library and Information Studies. She also served as the assistant curator of the de Grummond Collection from 1986 to 1991. She is coauthor of *Teaching Children's Literature* (McFarland, 1995).

DianeJude L. McDowell has served as head of the Children's Special Collections at The Free Library of Philadelphia since 1993 and was the assistant head from 1982 to 1986.

Margaret Maloney was curator of the Osborne Collection of Early Children's Books, the Lillian H. Smith and Canadiana Collections of the Toronto Public Library. She is an author, editor, lecturer, and consultant. In 1992, the University of New Brunswick recognized her contribution to the field of children's literature with a Doctor of Laws, *honoris causa.*

Linda Murphy is a former curator of the Alice M. Jordan Collection at the Boston Public Library (1987 to 1992). She is secretary of the Foundation for Children's Books, a literature and literacy advocacy group in Newton, Massachusetts. Currently, she is employed as a school librarian in Canton, Massachusetts.

Justin G. Schiller has spent more than forty years working within the field of rare and collectible children's books, both as a private collector and then as a dealer. He is a member of the Antiquarian Booksellers Association of America (since 1967), under whose auspices he began doing appraisals. He is currently preparing a millennium exhibition of significant milestones in children's literature for the Grolier Club (New York).

Zena Sutherland is professor emeritus of the Graduate Library School of the University of Chicago and former editor of *The Bulletin of the Center for Children's Books.* She is the author of *Children and Books* (New York: Addison, Wesley Longman, 1996, 9th ed.).

INDEX